rororo Sprachen

Herausgegeben von Ludwig Moos

Dieser Grammatikkurs ist für alle, die beim Englischlernen bislang nichts zu lachen hatten. *Joke Your Way Through English Grammar* folgt dem Prinzip "Lernen und Lächeln". Geübt wird auf zwei Levels, mit besonderem Augenmerk auf den spezifischen Problemen deutscher Sprachenlerner. Alle wichtigen Regeln sind in griffige Merksätze gefasst, als Übungsbeispiele dienen Jokes und witzige Zitate. Einprägsamer, weil merkwürdiger, lässt sich Grammatik kaum lernen.

Dr. René Bosewitz ist *native speaker* und leitet eine Sprachschule in Heidelberg. Bei rororo sprachen hat er *Better Your English* (60802), *Perfect Your English* (61147) und zusammen mit Robert Kleinschroth *Joke by Joke to Conversation* (8795) veröffentlicht sowie die Reihe Business English konzipiert und geschrieben.

Robert Kleinschroth unterrichtet Englisch am Gymnasium und an der Universität Heidelberg. Zusammen mit Dieter Maupai hat er *La Conversation en s'amusant* (8873) und *Flüssiges Französisch* (61184) verfasst und außerdem *Sprachen lernen* (9140) geschrieben.

René Bosewitz / Robert Kleinschroth

Joke Your Way Through English Grammar

Mit Pfiff und Witz zum
sicheren Gebrauch

Rowohlt Taschenbuch Verlag

Überarbeitete und erweiterte Neuausgabe, Oktober 2002
Veröffentlicht im Rowohlt Taschenbuch Verlag GmbH,
Reinbek bei Hamburg, Mai 1989
Copyright © 1989, 2002 by Rowohlt Taschenbuch Verlag GmbH,
Reinbek bei Hamburg
Umschlaggestaltung Notburga Stelzer
(Illustration Gerd Huss)
Layout Anne Drude
Satz Stone PostScript, QuarkXPress 4.11
Druck und Bindung Clausen & Bosse, Leck
Printed in Germany
ISBN 3 499 61408 1
Die Schreibweise entspricht den Regeln der neuen Rechtschreibung.

Table of Contents

Preface

*J*oke Your Way Through English Grammar ist ein Lern- und Arbeitsbuch für Fortgeschrittene und Wiedereinsteiger, die das Angenehme mit dem Nützlichen verbinden und in der Grammatik auf vergnüglichere Weise sicher werden wollen. Vielleicht kennen Sie unser altes *Joke Your Way*. In Deutschland war es wohl die erste 'ganz andere Grammatik' mit Regeln in Versen, mit Witzen als Beispielsätzen und Übungen.

Wir haben *Joke Your Way* komplett überarbeitet. Das Prinzip 'Lernen und Lächeln' haben wir beibehalten. Doch die Regeln sind klarer, kürzer und präziser. Dabei haben wir unser Augenmerk besonders auf die Probleme deutscher Sprachenlerner gerichtet. Wo immer möglich haben wir die typischen dürren Muster- und Übungssätze vermieden. Bei uns finden Sie ausgesuchte Beispiele angelsächsischen Humors.

Warum *jokes*, pfiffige Lebensweisheiten und kluge Zitate?

Wir haben etwas gegen die üblichen Grammatiksätze (auch wenn wir nicht ganz darauf verzichten konnten). Meist sind sie künstlich, konstruiert, banal, zusammenhangslos und deshalb nicht merkwürdig. Ein Witz dagegen ist eine komplette kleine Situation in lebendiger Umgangssprache. Oft ist die Pointe eine intellektuelle Herausforderung. Stellt sich das Aha-Erlebnis ein, wird man ihn sich einprägen und vielleicht weitererzählen. All dies machen Sie mit einem spröden Grammatiksatz bestimmt nicht.

Joke Your Way Through English Grammar hat fünf Teile:

1. den Lese- und Arbeitsteil mit 22 Kapiteln,
2. den Schlüssel zu den Übungen mit genauem Verweis auf die zutreffende Regel,
3. unser *Grammar ABC* mit anschaulichen Beispielen, in dem Sie nachschlagen können, falls Sie beispielsweise nicht mehr wissen, was der Unterschied zwischen *Indefinite Article* und *Definite Article* ist,
4. die unregelmäßigen Verben, die man einfach kennen muss,
5. und einen ausführlichen Wortschatzteil, der dafür sorgt, dass Sie alles verstehen.

Auch der Kapitelaufbau ist neu. Jedes Kapitel besteht aus fünf Teilen:

1. Der Eingangstest zeigt Ihnen, wie nötig das Kapitel für Sie ist oder ob Sie es überspringen können.
2. Der Grammatikteil ist in zwei *Levels* aufgeteilt: *Level I* enthält das Basiswissen, *Level II* die Feinheiten für weiter Fortgeschrittene.
3. Zu jedem Level finden Sie Übungen. Die Lösungen schlagen Sie im *Key* nach.
4. Nach den Übungen begegnen Ihnen die typischen Sprachfallen für Deutsche.
5. Durch das Buch begleitet uns Merlin, der legendäre Vorfahre Harry Potters. Seine wundersamen Erfahrungen im Deutschland des 21. Jahrhunderts bilden den Abschluss jeden Kapitels. Der lockere Text enthält in konzentrierter Form die Strukturen des jeweiligen Kapitels.

Wir wünschen Ihnen Freude und Erfolg bei der Lektüre.

Prologue

*O*nce upon a time there was a man of many magic *deeds.* | es war einmal,
His name was Merlin, the *magician* and spinner of | Tat; Zauberer
words. He was born or created – who knows it exactly –
many hundreds of years ago at the time of the druids. They
were some sort of strange people with special *magical* | Zauberkraft
powers. Merlin learned a lot from them. He could do magic
spells, turn boring high school teachers into *squeaking* rats, | quietschen
or drunken English teachers into *empty* bottles. But more | leer
than that, our mentor could travel through time, so don't
be *surprised* to find him here, there and everywhere. | überrascht
Of course, as time passed Merlin's magical powers *weak-* | schwach werden
ened, but he never lost the power of words, so to speak.
And, being a magician of good deeds and heart he decided
to help human beings everywhere (and any other crea-
tures) to perfect the language they spoke, the words and
forms they used so that they could present their ideas and
themselves in the best light. Merlin felt it his *task* in life to | Aufgabe
help the new masters of the earth to communicate, for in
communication is knowledge and hope, and without it
there is only frustration and *loneliness.* | Einsamkeit
And so it was with Merlin's work and *advice.* He was to help | Rat
with the bricks and the *mortar* of communication – the | Mörtel
words and the grammar.
Suddenly the room where the authors of this book were
working became darker and colder. Bob *moaned* to Ron, | klagen
"That's typical here in England in these *ancient* houses. | uralt
Electricity on the blink." Suddenly on the screen of their
oversized computer a face *appeared.* It was an old man with | überdimensioniert;
a white beard who looked angrily up at Ron. His old white | erscheinen
beard *trembled* and a tired but powerful voice came from | zittern
the machine. "Do not use words like grammar! This has a
negative touch to it. It takes the reader's mind back to un-
happy days at school. It kills his interest. Talk about langu-
age *links* or building stones or bridges or something else. | Brücken
Think in terms of communication. Think before you
write!" With that the wise old man faded from the screen.
Ron looked at Bob. "This might be more difficult than we
thought" he grumbled.

Der Imperativ – The Imperative

CHECK your Imperatives

Spot the mistake

a. Seien Sie vorsichtig!   Be ~~you~~ careful!
b. Reden wir übers Geschäft.   Let's talk business, will we?
c. Entweder oder.   Take ~~you~~ it or leave it!
d. Sei immer ehrlich!   Be always honest!

Tick them off

Right Wrong

a. Sit down, please.
b. Sit you down, will you.
c. Help yourself, please.
d. Don't sit down on this chair!
e. Don't sit you down on that chair!
f. Please, do wait for me.
g. Don't forget! You pay for me!

Time for a SMILE

In the supermarket a man was pushing a pram[1] with a screaming baby. The man kept repeating phrases like, "*Don't get excited*, Albert. *Don't scream*[2], Albert. *Keep calm*, Albert." A woman standing next to him said, "It's fantastic how you're looking after little Albert." The man turned round and then he said quietly, "Madam, I am Albert."

1 Kinderwagen   2 schreien

Der Imperativ

LEVEL I : Das Einmaleins des Imperativs

1

Der bejahte Imperativ

1. *Do* me a favour!	Tu / Tun Sie / Tut mir einen Gefallen!
2. *Keep* running!	Lauf / Laufen Sie / Lauft weiter!
3. *Be* careful!	Sei / Seien Sie / Seid vorsichtig!
4. *Have* a seat.	Nimm / Nehmen Sie / Nehmt Platz!
5. *Rest* in peace.	Ruhe in Frieden!

✪ Der bejahte Imperativ hat die Form des Infinitivs.
✪ Achtung: eine Form im Englischen – drei mögliche Übersetzungen im Deutschen. Der Zusammenhang entscheidet.

Der verneinte Imperativ

6. *Don't* be stupid!	Sei / Seien Sie / Seid nicht dumm!
7. *Do not* shout!	Schrei / Schreien Sie / Schreit nicht so!
8. *Don't* worry!	Mach / Machen Sie sich / Macht euch keine Sorgen!

✪ Durch vorangestelltes *Do not / Don't* verneint man den Imperativ.

Der Imperativ drückt also aus:

Bitten (1)	Befehle (2, 7)	Anweisungen (2)	Warnungen (3)
Einladungen (4)	Wünsche (5)	Missfallen (6)	Ratschläge (8)

Time for a SMILE

"Don't worry," a patient told his psychiatrist. "I'll pay every penny I owe, or my name isn't Alexander the Great!"

Merlins *Merlins* Zwischenprüfung

A. Translate the words in brackets.

Advice to taxpayers: (*Arbeiten Sie*) hard and for many hours, (*versuchen Sie*) to be honest, and you'll be the darling of the Inland Revenue Office[1].

1

B. Which of the following sentences is best?

1.
a. Decide what your level of English is and tick the box.
b. Decide what your level of English is and tick you the box.
c. Decide what your level of English is and could you tick the box?
2.
d. Not send off the letter until you've signed it.
e. Don't send you off the letter until you've signed it.
f. Don't send off the letter until you've signed it.

C. Best word for the gap! (*machen* und *sparen*)

Graffiti: _____ love not war!

_____ energy. _____ love more slowly!

D. Translate the German in the brackets.

1. Patient: Shall I start at the beginning?
   Doctor: (*Tun Sie das, bitte*).
   Patient: Well ...... In the beginning I created Heaven and Earth.

2. (*Erzählen Sie nicht*) your friends about your indigestion.
   "How are you?" is a greeting, not a question.

E. Complete the Imperative.

1. _____ tell lies when you can use statistics.
2. Sign in a German bar for British soldiers: _____worry how bad our English is. Our Scotch is excellent.

---

1 Finanzamt

LEVEL II : Tipps für Kenner

1

9. Voranstellung von **Do**..., **Never** ..., **Always** ... verstärkt eine Bitte:

Road safety notice outside a school:
Drive carefully! Don't kill a child.
Do wait for the teachers!

Advice to salesmen:
Never simply say: "Sorry, we don't have what you are looking for." – *Always* say: "Too bad, I just sold the last one today."

10. Nachgestelltes **will you?** / **would you?** lässt Aufforderungen höflicher klingen:

Doctor to Lady: And if these pills don't cure your kleptomania, *try and get* me a video recorder, *will you*?

11. Mit vorangestelltem **Let's / Let us** bezieht man sich in den Befehl mit ein. Nachgestelltes **shall we?** erhöht die Dringlichkeit.

Max entered the psychiatrist's rooms and settled himself down on the couch with his briefcase. *"Let's talk business, shall we?"* he said. "I want to rent advertising space on your ceiling."

12. Vorangestelltes **You** oder **Don't you** klingt energisch, bedrohlich:

Tom: *Don't you pull* faces at my parrot! He's very sensitive.
Bob: All right, but he started it!

"Let's get one thing straight," the bride said to her future husband. "I'm not cleaning up after you. I'm a career woman. That means I pay other people to do housework. Got it?"
"How much?"
"Eight dollars an hour. *You take it or leave it!*"

Merlins *Merlins* Reifeprüfung

F. Time for a *woggle*. Replace the *woggle* with the correct form.

1. He: I'd like to make your dreams come true.
   She: *Woggle* you try, or I'll slap your face.
2. Ron: Tell me why people take an instant dislike to me, *woggle* you!
   Bob: I'd say they want to save time.
3. Husband to wife: If it's a boy, let's call him John, *woggle* we? If it's a girl, we could call her Jane, couldn't we? And if it's twins, *woggle* call it a day.

1

G. Complete the following by selecting from the boxes below.
Use the ideas in box C or make combinations from A + C or B + C.
The first one has been done for you.

> Do
> Do not
> Don't

> tell me about it / forget your key
> help yourself / go somewhere else
> turn off the electricity supply
> go for a walk / say I'm out /
> disturb

> Let's

1. OK, everyone. There's plenty to eat and drink, so *do help yourselves*!
2. I'm tired of staying indoors. I need some fresh air.
   _____ .
3. I'll be in bed when you come home, so _____ .
4. It sounds terribly exciting! _____ !
5. Examination in progress. _____ .
6. _____ before repairing the machine.
7. I'm busy, so if anyone phones, please _____ .
8. I'm fed up with going to discos. _____ for a change, shall we?

Der Imperativ

13. Satzzeichen

✪ Imperative in normalem Tonfall enden mit einem Punkt.

✪ Ausrufezeichen deuten an, dass der Imperativ mit Nachdruck und erhobener Stimme gesagt wird.

✪ ... *will you?* mit Fragezeichen mildert, ... *will you!* mit Ausrufezeichen verstärkt den Imperativ.

✪ Tom, don't play with the dog. – Tom doesn't play with the dog.
Mit Komma: Befehl (*don't*) – Ohne Komma: Aussage (*doesn't*)

SPRACHFALLEN  für Deutsche

Deutsch	Falsch	Englisch
1. Kommen Sie herein!	*Come you in.*	Come in.
2. Setzen Sie sich bitte.	*Sit yourself down.*[1]	Sit down, please.
3. Raus mit dir / Ihnen / euch.	*(Beachte die drei Möglichkeiten.)*	Get out of here!
4. Bedient euch!	*Help yourself.*	Help *yourselves*!

✪ Zu 1: Das *Sie / Du* bleibt unübersetzt

✪ Zu 2: Einem deutschen Reflexivpronomen entspricht nicht immer ein englisches Reflexivpronomen (sich, dich, euch: *yourself, yourselves*).

✪ Zu 3: Vorsicht bei Übersetzung ins Deutsche. Der englische Imperativ ist mehrdeutig. Es gibt nur eine Form, sei es für eine Person oder eine Gruppe, ganz gleich, ob man sie duzt oder siezt.

✪ Zu 4: Das Reflexivpronomen macht es deutlich, ob eine oder mehrere Personen angesprochen werden.

---

1 existiert aber in der Umgangssprache

Merlin's saga

Ron wanted to *lose weight*, so he did a ten-mile jog. After that he *weighed* himself. He was even heavier than before the run. Now he was sitting in a Greek restaurant drinking strong white wine and trying to *drown* his *sorrows*. Little by little a face began to *appear* in his wine. Surprise, surprise, it was the old man.
"What you are doing is stupid. **Keep on** doing sport, certainly, but **do** it for fun and not for losing weight." "Who the devil are you?" *spluttered* Ron. "**Let's say** I'm a friend and an *adviser*, **shall we**? **Do as I say** and you will *improve* your life and your communication *skills*." Ron was as nervous as nervous could be. "**Just explain** what you meant by saying I was stupid to go running, **will you**?" The wizard *sighed*. "**Do try** to listen to the *voice* of your body. It's telling you to stop it. What have you *achieved* with your sport? Feel your knees! They are in pain. And you're getting as round as a *barrel*." Ron was beginning to feel desperate. "**Tell me** what to do, **will you**?" "Okay, my son, I'll help you to help yourself. **Let's work out** a simple plan. It goes like this. First, **change** the type of sport. **Go swimming**, for example. **Don't stress** your *joints*! Never go jogging again! Next drink this *magic potion*. This will kill your appetite. **Take** it every time you want to eat. **Don't you ever forget** it! If you do all this you will become a more *pleasant* fellow and a slimmer one. **Feel** good with yourself again. And then you will begin to communicate with your *fellow humans* once more."
The wine had turned into a dark green liquid. He took a *sip*. True enough his hunger had gone. Three seconds later his meal arrived. "Oh my God, **take** it away, **will you**. I can't *face* food." Shocked the waitress *grumbled*, "I hope you can face the *bill*. You ordered it, so **pay it, will you**!"
Conclusion: every good diet will cost you!

abnehmen
wiegen

Sorgen ertränken
erscheinen

1

stottern
Ratgeber; verbessern; Fertigkeit

seufzen; Stimme erreichen

Fass

Gelenk
Zaubertrank

angenehm

Mitmensch

Schluck

Anblick ertragen; murren; Rechnung

CHE CK your verb forms

2

Spot the mistake

a. Dieser Käse riecht schrecklich.   This cheese is smelling awful.
b. Er hat den ganzen Tag gewartet.   He has waited all day long.
c. Es wird immer kälter hier.   It gets colder and colder here.
d. Er schläft. Wecke ihn nicht.   Don't wake him up. He sleeps.

Tick them off

Right Wrong

a. Listen! Are you hearing that noise?
b. I'm seeing my doctor tomorrow.
c. Beer or wine? What are you thinking?
d. Sorry, but I'm not understanding you.
e. I'm having a shower now.
f. I'm not having a car at the moment.
g. The tree has been standing there for 50 years.

Time for a SMILE

Pilot to airline passengers: "Ladies and gentlemen, I *have* some good news and some bad news. The bad news is that we *have* a hijacker on board. The good news is he *wants* to go to the French Riviera."

LEVEL I : Das Einmaleins des Aspect

Aspect heißt Sichtweise. Je nachdem, wie der Engländer eine Situation sieht, verwendet er die *Simple Form* oder *Progressive Form* des Verbs. Im Deutschen gibt es diese doppelte Sichtweise nicht.

2

Formen

Tense	Simple Form	Progressive Form
Present	Tim *plays* tennis well.	He *is playing* in Wales this week.
Present Perfect	He *has* even *trained* a German tennis team.	He *has been training* tennis teams for years.
Past	Tim *started* to train our team last year.	We *were playing* badly when Tim became our coach.
Past Perfect	We *had lost* four matches before Tim arrived.	To be honest, we *had been losing* for years.

Globalregel[1]

1. Simple Forms für Dauerzustände und oft wiederholte Vorgänge.

Der Neckar fließt in den Rhein.	The Neckar *flows* into the Rhine.
Tom schreibt Romane.	Tom *writes* novels.

2. Progressive Forms für zeitlich begrenzte Zustände und Vorgänge, die zu einem Zeitpunkt im Verlauf, das heißt nicht abgeschlossen sind.

Der Neckar fließt *heute* schnell.	The Neckar is *flowing* rapidly today.
Tom schreibt (*gerade*) einen Brief an seine Freundin.	Tom *is writing* a letter to his girlfriend.

1 Detaillierte Regeln finden Sie bei den verschiedenen Zeiten.

Merlins Merlins Zwischenprüfung

A. Do you know the forms when you see them? Name them and say why they are used.

2

1. "I don't want you to use those bad words again."
   "But mother, Shakespeare often uses them."
   "Well, don't play with him again."

2. René: Stop acting like a fool, Robert.
   Robert: But *I'm* not *acting*.

B. Put in the correct form of the verb.

Tim Jones and Anita Plod work at the reception desk of U.B.M. Copiers.
Tim (*explain*) the latest copier model to Anita:
Anita: How you (*work*) this photocopier? I think I (*do*) something wrong.
Tim: Yes, you (*press*) the wrong button. That one (*enlarge*) the
        copies. You need to press this one.
Anita: Oh yes. It (*work*) properly now.

C. Which is correct?

1. Guest: Waiter, what *does this fly / is this fly* doing in my soup?
   Waiter: Breast-stroke, I suppose.
2. I sold the memoirs of my sex life to a publisher this morning.
   They *make / are making* a board game out of it. (WOODY ALLEN)

D. Is it live or living? Fit in the right form.

1. San Francisco is the only place where a working-class man _____
   like a queen.
2. I _____ so far beyond my income that we may almost be said to
   _____ apart.
3. The interior decorator installed a skylight in my apartment. The
   people who _____ above me are furious!
4. "I really don't want a lot of money," said Tina . "I just wish we
   could afford to live the way we _____ now."

LEVEL II : Tipps für Kenner

2

Statische und dynamische Verben

3. **Dynamische Verben** stehen im Progressive.
   Der Engländer wählt diese Form, wenn er sich Handlungen oder Vorgänge in ihrem Verlauf vorstellt. Dies kann er in der Regel nur bei dynamischen Verben wie
   a. Tätigkeitsverben: *do, make, work, run, play, write* etc.
   b. Vorgangsverben: *become, grow, get*

4. **Statische Verben** stehen im Simple Tense.
   a. Zustandsverben: *be, have, contain, belong, possess, own, need*
   b. Verben, die eine Eigenschaft bedeuten und durch *be* ersetzt werden könnten: *taste good, smell awful, look fine, feel like silk, seem good, cost money*
   c. Verben der Sinneswahrnehmung: *see, hear, notice, mind*
   d. Verben des Wissens, Glaubens, Meinens: *believe, expect (= think), know, mean, think, understand*

Spezialfälle

5. Manche statische Verben können im Progressive stehen und erhalten dadurch eine andere, eine dynamische und zeitlich begrenzte Bedeutung. Vergleichen Sie:

You *are* silly.	Du bist albern.
You're *being* silly (today).	Du benimmst dich (heute) albern.
He's *tasting* the soup.	Er schmeckt die Suppe ab.
The soup *tastes* (*is*) sour.	Die Suppe schmeckt (ist) sauer.
He's *seeing* Tina *off*.	Er begleitet Tina zur Tür[1].
I don't *see* the difference.	Ich kann den Unterschied nicht erkennen.

1 Bedeutungsänderung bei *to see: see someone off* = sich von jemandem verabschieden; *see one's doctor:* seinen Arzt aufsuchen

Merlins Reifeprüfung

E. Choose the right one.

1. An expert is one who *knows / is knowing* more and more about less and less.
2. An optimist *believes / is believing* that what's going on will be postponed.
3. Young man: Are you *thinking / do you think* you could be happy with a man like me?
   Young woman: Of course! As long as he wasn't too much like you.

F. Match the rules to the example sentences.

1. Bob *is having* his breakfast in the garden.
2. The answer *seems* to be correct, but I'm not sure.
3. I *know* what you're telling me.
4. Why *are you smelling* that meat? It's okay.

A. Verben, die eine Eigenschaft bedeuten
B. Verben des Wissens, Glaubens, Meinens
C. Verb mit dynamischer Bedeutung
D. Spezialfall, Bedeutungswechsel

G. Translate the German in the brackets.

1. Ortrud: Manfred?
   Manfred: Yes, love.
   Ortrud: (*Ich glaube*) I'd like to be cremated.
   Manfred: Okay, love – get your coat on.

2. Bob: (*Glaubst du*) in ghosts?
   René: I don't, but I know they are there, and I (*vermute*) they don't believe in me, either.

3. What (*bekommst du*) if you (*kreuzt*) a terrier with a fire?
   A hot dog!

H. Progressive or Simple?

A: Good morning. Is Mr. Kleinstück in?

B: Yes, he is, but he _____ (*see*) someone at the moment.
He _____ (*expect*) you?

A: Yes, I _____ (*have*) an appointment with him at 10:30.
My name's Bossybitch.

B: Ah yes, Mr Bossybitch. I'm afraid we _____ (*run*) a little late
this morning, but I _____ (*not expect*) Mr Kleinstück will be
long, if you _____ (*not mind*) waiting.

2

SPRACHFALLEN für Deutsche

Deutsch	Falsch	Englisch
1. Schau, er schläft.	*Look, he sleeps.*	Look, he's *sleeping.*
2. Tom war Autor, er schrieb Romane.	*Tom was an author, he was writing novels.*	Tom was an author, he *wrote* novels.
3. Die Suppe schmeckt gut.	*The soup is tasting good.*	The soup *tastes* good.
4. Das Hotel gehört nun mir.	*The hotel is belonging to me now.*	The hotel *belongs* to me now.

✪ Zu 1: Zum Zeitpunkt des Sprechens läuft die Tätigkeit noch ab. Selbst Nichtstun ist für den Engländer dynamisch: *sleep, rest, lie, stand, wait.* (Level II: 3)

✪ Zu 2: Bücherschreiben war Toms Hobby oder Beruf, also eine oft wiederholte Tätigkeit. (Level I: 1)

✪ Zu 3: Die Suppe schmeckt gut, das heißt, sie *ist* gut. Eigenschaften und Zustände stehen nicht im Progressive. (Level II: 4)

✪ Zu 4: *The hotel belongs to me* beschreibt einen Zustand. (Level II: 4a)

Die einfachen Zeiten und ihre Verlaufsform

Merlin's saga

2

Merlin **knew** he had to *adapt himself* to life in the twenty-first century in Europe and in particular in Germany. That could be quite difficult as Merlin had been brought up in Brittania over the sea. There, they not only **speak** a different language, they also **have** a different way of thinking.	*sich anpassen*
"Okay," **though**t Merlin, "**I'll dress** myself in these *ugly* clothes, but I'm going to keep my long white beard." And so it **was** that (here in the centre of the modern world, Heidelberg), from time to time an old man could be seen in a *worn-out* suit *limping* along the street. One day he was stopped by a rosy-faced young fellow dressed in a green suit. He **had** an unfriendly smile. "Hey, you *tramp*, why **don't you go** to the Railway Station Mission and get something to eat? Then get a job and earn your way!"	*hässlich* *abgetragen; hinken* *Bettler*
"Sir, I **have** a job. I **have** a *vocation*. I am to help modern man to improve his ways before it is too late." The "*green bottle*" was angry. "When **did you last do** a day's work? What **do you** *contribute* to our society? Why, I think you are not even from here. Where **do you come from**?"	*Berufung* *hier: Polizist* *beitragen*
Merlin **remained** calm. "Sir, **I am living** here at present, but I am from foreign parts. You should not judge a book by its cover." The green uniform **was becoming** ruder. "Books? You have never seen a book from the inside. That's for sure."	*bleiben*
"Sir, be peaceful, or I may *turn* you *into* a green frog." The green person **put** his hand into his pocket. "**I'm arresting you** for *insulting* the "office" of an official. Now, what did you say your name was?"	*verwandeln* *beleidigen*

CHECK your Present Tenses

 Spot the mistake

a. During the dance the blonde says to her partner, "I dance a tango, and you?"
b. A professor is someone who is talking in someone else's sleep.
c. What we are calling work, the Mexicans call siesta.
d. A vegetarian is someone who eats vegetables not because he loves animals, but because he is hating plants.
e. If it's stinking, it's chemistry. If it doesn't work, it's physics.

 Tick them off

	Right	Wrong
a. Whenever I get home from office my wife is usually watching TV.		
b. Your problem is that you're always wishing for something you don't have.		
c. Why on earth do you always park your car in front of our gate?		
d. Inflation is when wallets are getting bigger and shopping bags smaller.		
e. A wise man is never laughing at his wife's old clothes.		
f. The Neckar is flowing into the river Rhine.		

Time for a SMILE

Two old soldiers *are talking*.
"Do you *remember* those pills they used to give us in the army to keep our minds off girls?" said one.
"Vaguely," said the other.
"Well," said the first, "I think *they are beginning* to work."

LEVEL I : Das Einmaleins des Präsens

3

Mit dem Simple Present sprechen wir über

1. Dauerzustände. Statische Verben stehen ebenfalls im Simple Present.	Everyone *wants* to go to Heaven – but nobody *wants* to die.
2. Naturgesetze und allgemeingültige, zeitlose Tatsachen.	We *live* in a world that is governed by Einstein's physics and Frankenstein's logic. (B. RUSSEL)
3. typische Fähigkeiten und Eigenschaften.	If it *wriggles*, it's biology. If it *stinks*, it's chemistry. If it *doesn't work*, it's physics.
4. Berufe, Hobbys und das, was man aus Gewohnheit oft, immer oder nie tut (mit *always, usually, sometimes, never ...*).	My husband *always remembers* my age, but *always forgets* my birthday.

Mit dem Present Progressive sprechen wir über

5. Vorgänge, Handlungen, die zum *Zeitpunkt* des Sprechens noch andauern (*now, at the moment, today, this year ...*)	During the dance the blonde says to her partner, *"I'm dancing a tango, and you?"*

Time for a SMILE

An old Japanese General and an American diplomat *are talking.* "Why do you *always win* battles whereas we *always lose* our wars?" wondered the Japanese General. – "Because we *always pray* to God before we go into battle," replies the diplomat. – "That's not so, because we also *pray* to God, but we *never win.*" – "Ah!" says the diplomat, "but not everyone can understand Japanese."

Merlins **Merlins** Zwischenprüfung

A. Choose the correct Aspect in the following.

The plane *circles / is circling* at ten thousand feet, the newly recruited Friesian parachutes *get / are getting* ready for their first jump. "Stop!" shouts the officer. "You *don't wear / are not wearing* your parachute." – "It's okay, captain," replies one of them. "Sure, it's only a practice jump we *do / are doing.*"

3

B. Select the correct Aspect.

1. Overheard in a pub:
   "I'm the boss in my house alright. My wife never *tells / is telling* me how to wash the dishes."

2. Money *doesn't always bring / isn't always bringing* happiness. A man with twenty million dollars isn't any happier than a man with one million.

C. Translate the German into English.

1. Women's faults are many. Men (*haben*) only two. Everything they (*sagen*) and everything they (*tun*).
2. "Please keep quiet, Robert! Your father (*versucht, möchte*) to read."

D. Put the verbs in the box into the following sentences.

> **look, want, try, reveal**

1. A study of economics usually _____ that the best time to buy anything is last year.
2. Teacher: Today we _____ to do without our calculators. What are 3 x 7?
   Pupil: When are we to hand in the result?
3. "You _____ for work, young man?" "No, but I wouldn't mind a job."
4. Dad: You _____ any help with your maths homework?
   Son: No thanks! I can get it wrong on my own.

LEVEL II : Tipps für Kenner

3

Simple Present für

6. Besprechung von Literatur, Filmen etc.	Hamlet's uncle *kills* Hamlet's father and *marries* his mother. So Hamlet *kills* his uncle, his future father-in-law, his mother, his friend etc.
7. Umgangssprachliche, lebhafte Aufzählung von Ereignissen.	Two Finnish friends *meet* up for a drink. After a long silence Dag *looks* up and *says:* "Well, how are you Matti?" To which Matti *replies*, "Look, did we come here to talk or to drink?"

Present Progressive bei Gewohnheiten

8. zum Ausdruck von Missbilligung in Verbindung mit Häufigkeitsadverbien (*always, continually, constantly, forever*). Vergleiche Level I: 4.	Father: Your problem is that *you're always wishing* for something you don't have. Son: But what else is there to wish for?
9. Sonderfall: Eine gewohnheitsmäßige Handlung (*get*) unterbricht einen bereits andauernden Vorgang (*watching*).	Whenever I get home from the office my wife *is* usually *watching* TV.

Time for a SMILE

I don't mind people looking at their watches when *I'm making* a speech, but it is damned disconcerting to see them shaking them to check if they *are* still *going*.

Merlins **Merlins** **Reifeprüfung**

E. Put the verbs in the brackets in the correct Tense.

A blonde (*be*) tired of hearing blond jokes and (*decide*) to prove people wrong. She (*spend*) weeks studying a map of the United States, and (*memorise*) all the capitals of all the states.

3

The next time someone started telling a blonde joke she said, "Hey, not all blondes are stupid. I can prove it. Give me the name of any state and I'll tell you its capital[1]." – "Vermont," someone suggested. Without hesitating she replied: "V".

F. Find the English.

The German is given in the box to help you.

> **wecken, schicken, verstehen, immer**

"I don't think Dad _____ much about children." – "Why do you say that?" – "Because he _____ me to bed when I'm wide awake and _____ me up when I'm sleepy."

G. Spot the mistakes and explain your corrections.

Good advice isn't easy to follow:
Bill and Kathy have gone to see their vicar for some marriage counselling. After talking to them for a while the vicar is getting up and hugging Kathy, then sits down. He then is getting up again and hugs Kathy a second and third time, before turning to Bill "Did you see that, Bill? Kathy is needing that every single day!"
"That's all very well, father," said Bill, "but I can only bring her over on Tuesdays and Thursdays."

H. Put in the correct Tense.

1. Bob always (*drink*) a drop of champagne before his evening meal. He says it's good for his blood.
2. Ron always (*go*) jogging before breakfast. He's trying to lose weight.

---

1 *capital* hat doppelte Bedeutung: a) Hauptstadt, b) großer Anfangsbuchstabe

3. Bob frequently (*tell*) Ron to stop wasting his time and energy. That's not the way to get thinner.
4. Ron is getting angry with Bob. "You always (*give*) me your good advice, but you don't do anything yourself."
5. Bob grumbled, "You constantly (*moan*) about your body. I just want to help."

3

SPRACHFALLEN für Deutsche

		Deutsch	Falsch	Englisch
1. Action now		Im Moment schreibt Bryan sein drittes Buch.	*Bryan now writes his third book.*	Bryan is *now writing* his third book.
2. Repeated action		Er geht jeden Tag ins Wirtshaus.	*He is going to the pub every day.*	He *goes* to the pub *every day*.
3. Stative verbs		Annette möchte China besuchen.	*Annette is wanting to visit China.*	Annette *wants* to visit China.
4. Always + criticism		Du streitest dich aber auch ständig mit mir!	*You always argue with me.*	You're *always arguing* with me!

✪ Zu 1: *Write* ist ein dynamisches Verb. Zum Zeitpunkt des Sprechens (*now*) hat die Tätigkeit *schon begonnen* und ist *noch nicht beendet*, deshalb Present Progressive.

✪ Zu 2: Er geht *regelmäßig, aus Gewohnheit* ins Pub, deshalb Present Simple.

✪ Zu 3: *Want* ist ein statisches Verb, deshalb Simple Present.

✪ Zu 4: Present Progressive trotz *always*, wenn emotionale Kritik zum Ausdruck gebracht wird.

Merlin's saga

Well, **do you remember** Ron from earlier chapters and his friend Bob? Bob, of course is a teacher, and teachers have pupils, and pupils have exams, and so it was. *Imagine* it! There is an exam, pupils **are sitting** around with *tears* in their eyes and heads *bent over*. And one **passes** answers to his friend on a secret sheet of paper. It is *hidden* between two slices of bread (which is the candidate's second breakfast). The two pupils are called Tom and Mick. Tom **passes** the bread to Mick. Mick **is looking** at the answer when he suddenly **hears** a *voice* in his head, tired but sharp. "At the moment **you are taking** an exam. **You are writing** the test to show how much you know. Later the teachers will *compare* you with your friends." Mick **becomes** nervous and angry. "Who are you in my head?" Merlin's voice is *peaceful*. "Mick, **we are living** in a world that is full of lies and swindling. This **destroys** a man's character. Such a person is the living dead. **Do you want** to *lose* your soul?" Mick **feels** *challenged*. "Tom has been my friend for years. Of course he will help me." – "How **do you feel** that you are swindling your other friends in the class?" "It **doesn't interest me**." The *wizard's* head went red. He **tries** to keep control, but *in vain*. "Then see if this interests you. Peno dryo nothing raito!" And poor Mick tried everything. He could not put a word on paper. Bob, the teacher came to him at the end of the exam. "Mick, what's wrong? Your page is *empty*."

sich vorstellen
Tränen
nach vorne gebeugt; versteckt

Stimme

vergleichen

friedlich

verlieren
herausgefordert

Zauberer
vergebens

leer

3

Über die Vergangenheit reden – Talking about the Past

CHECK your Past Tenses

Spot the mistake

a. Formerly Ron has weighed 95 kilos.
b. I have visited Ron in Battle during my autumn holidays.
c. When I arrived at his cottage, Ron worked in the garden.
d. Anne didn't know that I was coming, but she was cooking me a fine meal when I arrived.
e. And every night Ron was making a fire in the open fireplace.
f. Anne got a bottle of wine, Ron got the glasses and I was opening the bottle.

Tick them off

Right Wrong

a. Where have you met Ron?
b. I met him in Hollerberg.
c. He was shooting at the robber. The man was dead immediately.
d. Ron was inviting me to his cottage the other day.
e. I used to be a werewolf, but I'm all right nooooooooooow!

Time for a SMILE

The lifeguard was giving a young lady the kiss of life when her husband arrived.
"What are you doing to my wife?"
"I'm giving her artificial respiration, sir."
"Artificial?! Give her the right thing. I'll pay for it."

Level I : Das Einmaleins des Vergangenheit

4

Simple Past steht fast immer

1. nach Zeitangaben der Vergangenheit: *yesterday, last month, a week ago, the other day* (neulich).	"My father *died in the Second World War*. He was a Pole." "North or South?"
2. bei Situationen, die in der Vergangenheit abgeschlossen wurden.	I'm very proud of my golden pocket watch. My grandfather, on his death bed, *sold* it to me. (WOODY ALLEN)
3. bei Situationen, die in der Vergangenheit regelmäßig wiederkehrten.	Eve was so jealous of Adam that *each night* when he came home she *counted* his ribs.
4. bei aufeinander folgenden Situationen (Handlungsketten).	"We did the washing-up for you, Mum. Dad *washed*, Paul *wiped* and I *picked* up the pieces."

Past Progressive steht für

5. Aktivitäten, die zu einem Zeitpunkt schon, gerade oder noch im Verlauf waren.	Actually there were four wise men. *While they were following* the star on the way to Bethlehem, one of them said he knew a short cut.
6. eine gerade ablaufende allmähliche Entwicklung, einen Prozess in der Vergangenheit.	A man was on the point of being executed by the firing squad. "Would you like a last cigarette?" – "No," replied the man. "I *was trying* to give up."

Merlins Zwischenprüfung

4

A. Put in the correct tense.

1. My mother (*have*) a terrible accident the other day. She (*have*) the right of way, but the other guy had the truck.
2. "Sorry I'm late, sir. I (*sprain*) my ankle when I (*come*) downstairs." – "Huh! Another lame excuse!"
3. No woman has ever shot her husband while he (*do*) the dishes.

B. Translate the German in the brackets.

1. Bob: What (*passieren*) to that shockproof, waterproof, unbreakable, anti-magnetic watch I (*kaufen*) you for your last birthday?
   Ron: I lost it.

2. Eric: My father was very disappointed when I (*geboren werden*).
   Ernie: Why? Did he (*wollen*) a girl?
   Eric: No, he (*wollen*) a divorce.

3. A car (*fahren*) at 150 miles per hour on the motorway when it was stopped by the police. "Sorry, officer, was I driving too fast?" "No, sir. But you (*fly*) too low."

C. Find the correct form.

1. A small boy *was standing / stood* next to an escalator. He *was looking / looked* at the handrail.
   "Is there something wrong?" asks a shop assistant. "No, I was *just waiting / just waited* for my chewing gum to come back."

2. God was a woman until she *was changing / changed* her mind.

3. Ron: How *were you getting / did you get* that splinter in your finger?
   Bob: All I *was doing / did* was scratch my head.

LEVEL II : Tipps für Kenner

4

Simple Past steht

7.	in Fragen und Antworten über die Vergangenheit mit *when* und *where*.	Ron: Mum, Bob broke a window. Mum: That bad boy! *How did he do it?* Ron: I *threw* a stone and he *moved* out of the way
8.	für abgelegte Gewohnheiten und Gegensätze zwischen gestern und heute (oft mit *used to* = früher).	Tina: I *used to be* young once. Bill: Wow! What a memory! "I don't think I look 35, do you?" she asked her husband. "No, I don't," he said "but you *used to.*"

Past Progressive *kann* stehen

9.	für Hintergrund und Begleitumstände.	An amateur string quartet *was playing* Brahms last night. Brahms lost.
10.	für parallele, gleichzeitige Aktivitäten.	Well, I *was working*. She *was watching* a stupid TV programme.
11.	wenn man betonen will, wie die Zeit innerhalb eines Zeitraums verbracht wurde.	Doctor: Well, Mr Smith, you seem to be coughing much more easily this morning. Mr Smith, groaning in his bed: That's because I *was practising all night.*
12.	für Kritik an schlechten Gewohnheiten in Verbindung mit *always, never.*	Robert, you *were always arriv*ing late. That's why she divorced you.
13.	Erläuterungen, Entschuldigungen.	I *wasn't paying* attention. I'll be more careful in future.

Time for a SMILE

Little John: *I used to be* a big-game hunter. Why, for years I shot elephants in Alaska.
Big Alfred: That's impossible! There aren't any elephants in Alaska.
Little John: Of course not. I *shot* them all.

Merlins Reifeprüfung

4

D. Find the English for the German in brackets.

1. Have you noticed that all the things you (*pflegen zu tun*) when you were a kid are now being done by batteries?

2. What a mean person! She always (*heizen*) the knives so that we would use less butter.

3. In London a landlady explains to an American guest full of pride: Shakespeare (*pflegen zu schlafen*) in this bed. "Well," says the American, "you could at least have changed the sheets."

E. Build the questions

1. When ....?
   I started eating spicy food when I was fifteen.
2. When .... ?
   I went on my first date when I was eighteen.
3. Where ....?
   They had this silly idea at a pub in Heidelberg.

F. Find the mistakes.

1. Fred was asked how he got his black eye:
   "I taught my girlfriend the tango, we danced close together. Then her father came in. How was I to know he was stone deaf?"

2. I did a lot of running, but I was always getting injured, so I was giving it up.

3. An Englishman and an American were shipwrecked on an island. The natives were very friendly and after six months the American was running a light railway, while the Englishman still waited to be introduced.

SPRACHFALLEN  für Deutsche

4

Deutsch	Falsch	Englisch
1. Wo hast du ihn kennen gelernt?	*Where have you known him?*	Where did you meet him?
2. Wann bist du ange-kommen?	*When have you arrived?*	When *did* you *arrive*?
3. Früher war er Lehrer. Jetzt ist er Taxifahrer.	*He was a teacher in former times. Now he is a taxi driver.*	He *used to be* a teacher. Now he is a taxi driver.

- ✪ Zu 1: Simple Past – denkt man an einen Ort, an dem man nicht mehr ist, denkt man auch an den damaligen Zeitpunkt. (7)
- ✪ Zu 2: Die Ankunft muss sich komplett zu einem vergangenen Zeitpunkt ereignet haben, deshalb Simple Past. (7)
- ✪ Zu 3: abgelegte Gewohnheiten und Gegensatz zwischen gestern und heute: *used to*. (8)

Time for a SMILE

> The boss demanded to know where Tom had been.
> "I've been for a haircut."
> "You can't have your hair cut in office time!"
> "Why not? It grows in office time."
> "Not all of it," said the boss.
> "So I didn't have it all cut off," Tom replied.

Merlin's saga

4

Well, it was two days before Merlin finally **got out** of the *police station*. He **was** *furious*. "Why **did I travel** through time to waste my life on these *lager louts*?" he **moaned**. Merlin **limped** along to the railway station. "I **didn't eat** anything while I was at that police station. They simply **had no** manners. There are quite a few people in this inn here, what's its name – Macknogoods." Merlin **was entering** the "inn" when a young fellow **banged** into him spilling his chips and coke all over our time-travelling hero. "Here, watch where you're going, you old fool." Merlin **felt** his anger rising. "Sir, I **was walking** in a *straight line*, slowly maybe, but I **was doing** the right thing." His conversation partner **turned out** to be drunk. "Maybe you **used to have** a brain to guide you, but now you're over the hill. You can hardly get your words out." – "Get my words out? I'll get a few words out and you will wish I had never spoken."

The *ancient* wizard **whispered** "drip-di-drop-di-dooba." (He used to be a jazz wizard in younger years).

The lager lout stood still as if he had been *frozen* where he **was standing**. There he was, hamburger in hand, the ketchup running out, down his jacket, down his trousers. *What a mess*! And what's the bottom line? Don't frustrate a weary wizard! He might *turn* you red.

Polizeirevier; wütend; besoffene Rüpel

geradeaus

sich herausstellen

uralt; flüstern

einfrieren

was für eine Schweinerei!

verwandeln

CHECK your Present Perfect

5

Spot the mistake

a. An intellectual is a man who found something more interesting than women.
b. I live in Bonn for 20 years.
c. Paul and Pauline have known each other since three years.
d. When have you started to study?
e. I've met Peter at the station.
f. Bob has been failing his exam at least three times.
g. We've been in Rome on our 25th wedding anniversary.

Tick them off

Right Wrong

a. "Thank God! He has been passing his exam."
b. "What a mess!" – "Well, I've been painting the garage."
c. I repaired the car. You can continue your trip.
d. I live with my mother since Easter because my house burnt down a month ago.
e. We have known each other since school.
f. He has already been having three accidents.
g. I am waiting for you for three hours.

Time for a SMILE

A famous film star went into a shop in a small town.
"*Haven't I seen* you somewhere before?" asked the shop assistant.
"In the cinema, perhaps?" replied the film star with a smile.
"Maybe. Where do you usually sit?"

Level I : Das Einmaleins des Present Perfect

5

Present Perfect Simple drückt aus	
1. dass eine Situation in der Vergangenheit begonnen hat und bis zum Zeitpunkt des Sprechens andauert (besonders bei statischen Verben).	"Haven't I seen your face somewhere else?" – "I don't think so. It *has always been* between my ears."
2. dass sich etwas *bis jetzt, schon mal, mehrmals* oder *nie* ereignet hat (oft mit *ever, never, so far, yet, lately, recently, this morning / week, just, since, for*).	Of course I *have played* outdoor games. I once played dominoes in an open air café in Paris. Some pupils *have never cheated* during an exam.
3. dass ein Ergebnis vorliegt, das für die Gegenwart wichtig ist – ein Zeitpunkt bleibt unerwähnt.	They *have passed* a law to make attendance at the German Bundestag obligatory – by twelve votes to four.

Present Perfect Progressive steht	
4. für Vorgänge, die bis jetzt (eventuell auch noch in der Zukunft) andauern – oft bei Zeitangaben mit *how long, since* oder *for*	"You *have been wearing* the wedding ring on the wrong finger ever since I first met you." "I know. I married the wrong man."
5. für Serien *nicht abgezählter* Ereignisse, die bis zur Gegenwart andauern (siehe unten).	My mother-in-law *has been coming* round to our house at Christmas *every year*. This time we're thinking of letting her in.

✪ Zu 4: Die Verben der Ruhe: *sleep, rest, lie, sit* stehen häufig im Progressive. Sie versteht der Engländer nicht als statisch.

✪ Zu 4, 5: Das Present Perfect Progressive steht häufig nach Zeitangaben wie: *all day* (*long*), *for ages* (eine Ewigkeit), *the whole morning* sowie *since* (seit einem Zeitpunkt / Ereignis) und *for* (seit einem Zeitraum).

✪ Zu 5: Vergleiche *I've been writing letters all day long* und *I've written ten letters today*. Abgezählte Serien betonen das Ergebnis und stehen im Present Perfect Simple.

Merlins Zwischenprüfung

A. Identification game.

Look at our rules (1–3) and match the numbers (rules) to the sentences:

Level I: 1,   Level I: 2,   Level I: 3

5

1. Son: Dad, how soon will I be old enough to do as I please?
   Father: I don't know. Nobody has lived that long yet.
2. Thanks to the speed of modern jet travel, holiday-makers can now be sick in countries they have never even heard of before.
3. I've always been interested in girls. That's what has kept me young.

B. Find the English for the words in brackets.

1. What do you call a man who (*verlieren*) half of his brain?
   A widower.
2. "Darling, do you have a good memory for faces?" – "Yes, I think so. Why do you ask?" – "Because I just (*brechen*) your shaving mirror."
3. No one ever (*sich beklagen*) of a parachute not opening.

C. Which is best? Simple or Progressive?

1. My wife *has been missing / has been missed* for two days. I don't know whether she has left me or gone shopping.
2. After the baptism the vicar praises the parents: "I've never seen such a well-behaved baby." – "No wonder", says the proud father. "We*'ve been practising / we have practised* all week with a watering can."
3. A man bought a parrot at an auction after some very brisk bidding. "I hope this bird talks," he said to the auctioneer. "Does he talk?" "Who do you think *has been bidding / has bid against* you for the past twenty minutes?"
4. She *has taken / has been taking* fifty of these anti-fat pills. Now she's so thin that every time she walks in the park, a dog tries to bury her.

Das englische Perfekt

LEVEL II : Tipps für Kenner

5

Present Perfect Simple und Progressive – Vergleich

Present Perfect Simple	Present Perfect Progressive
6. Abgezählte Wiederholung: The telephone *has rung 4 times.*	7. Ungezählte Wiederholung: The telephone *has been ringing* all morning.
8. Was wurde bis jetzt erreicht? *I have written 7 letters* since this morning.	9. Wie wurde die Zeit verbracht? *I have been writing letters* for hours.
10. Ergebnis: *I've repaired* the car. We can leave immediately.	11. Entschuldigung für unbeabsichtigtes Ergebnis: My God! What have you done to my car? – Sorry, but I *have been trying* to repair it.

Spezialfall

Hot News: Aktuelle Neuigkeiten mit Konsequenzen für die Gegenwart können im Present Perfect stehen, auch wenn sie in der Vergangenheit stattfanden.	Did you hear / Have you heard the news? They *have shot* the President.

SPRACHFALLEN  für Deutsche

Deutsch	Falsch	Englisch
1. Ich habe ihn im Bus gesehen.	*I have seen him on the bus.*	I *saw* him on the bus.[1]
2. Ich habe ein Jahr in Bonn gelebt.	*I have lived in Bonn for a year.*	I lived in Bonn for a year.
3. Wartest du schon lange?	*Are you waiting (for) long?*	*Have* you *been waiting* (for) long?
4. Was hast du gesagt?	*What have you said?*	What *did* you *say?*

1 Die Begegnung *on the bus* muss in der Vergangenheit stattgefunden haben, wenn sich Sprecher und Zuhörer nicht mehr im Bus befinden.

Merlins Reifeprüfung

D. Spot the mistake.

1. "Mummy, you know that old vase in the hall? The one they handed down from generation to generation?" – "Yes." – "Well, this generation has been coming to apologise for dropping it."
2. "How long has old Pedro fished?" – "I'm not sure, but he's the only member of the angling club fishing with a Louis XV rod."
3. Teaching was ruining more American novelists than drink. (GORE VIDAL)

5

E. Which is correct?

1. I _____ seven pints of beer since lunchtime and now I'm as drunk as a lord.
   a. have been drinking   **b.** have drunk   **c.** drank
2. "Hey Jim, _____ Sue at the railway station? Her train was due at 7 p.m."
   a. have you seen   **b.** do you see   **c.** did you see
3. I can't understand the fuss over computer pornography. Surely everybody _____ a computer without clothes on by now.
   a. has seen   **b.** has been seeing   **c.** saw

F. How would you translate the German in the brackets?

1. The following advertisement (*erscheinen*) in a Scottish newspaper: A gentleman who (*verlieren*) a left leg would like to correspond with another who (*verlieren*) his right leg and takes a size nine shoe.
2. "Prisoner, this court (*anklagen*) you of stealing £5,000, but it has been unable to prove you guilty. Therefore, you are now free to go. Do you have anything to say?" – "(*Soll das heißen*) that I can keep the money?"

Merlin's Merlin's saga

5

For the moment Merlin *has had* enough of Germany. "I'll go back to old Engeland," he whispers. He **has been walking** the streets of Livingpool in Engeland searching for people to be helped to a better life. "After all, wasn't it here that modern music was born?" Merlin is dressed in local clothing, *scruffy* shoes, old jeans and a *chequered* shirt. He **has decided** to find out why so many people in Livingpool have no money, no job and nowhere to live. "It must be something written in their stars," thought the old *wizard*. "I'll visit the Job Centre for work to see where the problems are. Perhaps I can help." Later at the *Job Centre* Merlin tried to *interview* the clerk.

schmuddelig; kariert

Zauberer
Arbeitsamt
ein Gespräch führen

"So I've come here to talk about work, to find out what's *going wrong*." The clerk, who **has been having** a very difficult day, was not particularly *sensitive* to Merlin's problems. He spoke out his questions mechanically. "*Surname*, first name, address in that order, please." – "Merlin **has been** my name for more centuries than I can remember. My *place of residence* is the earth of the New Age." The clerk was uninterested. "Well, that's a new line, I *suppose.* How long **have you lived** in Livingpool? How long **have you been** at this address?" Merlin was a little *confused.* "Time is a difficult concept. I'**ve always had** problems with it. Three of your weeks, I think." – "Oh it's like that, is it? Well, I can't find any *record* of you. How long **have you been living** on *unemployment benefit*?" Merlin was *mystified.* "I **have never been** unemployed. I **have always worked**, and only for the good of people. For centuries I **have been saving** people from themselves."

schief gehen
empfänglich
Nachname

Wohnsitz
annehmen

verwirrt

Akte
Arbeitslosengeld
verblüfft

The clerk was *undisturbed*. "So, if I **have understood** correctly, you have experience in social work?"–"Yes, I'**ve had** some centuries of *experience* in that, if you want to *put it like that.*"

ungerührt
Erfahrung
sozusagen

Imperfekt und Perfekt im Vergleich
Past and Present Perfect compared

CHECK your Tenses

CHECK

Spot the mistake

a. Why has Australia got all the Kangaroos and Austria all the Austrians? –
God has given the Australians the first choice.
b. After man came woman. And she was after him ever since.
c. Ron: I thought you are on a diet, Bob.
Bob: I am. But I have already had my diet and now I'm having my dinner.
d. Baker: I have been making bread before you were born.
Customer: Maybe so, but why are you selling it now?

Tick them off

Right Wrong

a. The Pentagon once has paid $435 for a hammer
available for $7 in the shops.
b. I already received ten compliments today. Two of them
were from other people.
c. In 1703 the Irish invented the toilet seat.
In 1704 the English put a hole in it.
d. I've met a Japanese gentleman who was so wealthy that
he wanted to buy what he called 'a place down South'.
It was Australia.

Time for a SMILE

There was a terrible fog in Ireland. Two drivers collided.
They groped their way out of their cars and approached each other.
"I had right of way!" says the first.
"Possibly, but it doesn't matter," replies the other. "We're in my garage."

LEVEL I : Der kleine Unterschied

6

Present Perfect Simple	Simple Past
1.	
I've *read* this book and I *find* it fascinating.	I *read* this book *last week* and I *found* it fascinating.
Das Ergebnis ist wichtig und nicht der Zeitpunkt des Lesens. Eine Zeitangabe wird nicht genannt.	Die Zeitangabe der Vergangenheit wird genannt (oder ergibt sich aus dem Kontext).
2.	
Have you *ever been* to Paris? Yes, I've *often been* there.	When *did* you *first go* there? *When* I *was* 18.
Etwas hat sich *schon mal, mehrmals, oft* oder *nie* bis zum Zeitpunkt des Sprechens ereignet.	Häufig in Fragen nach Zeitpunkt (*when?*) oder Ort (*where?*), an dem sich etwas ereignet hat.
3.	
Have you *seen* Tom *this year?* – No, I *haven't.*	I s*aw* Tom twice *in Berlin* this year.
Etwas ist in einem Zeitraum, der noch andauert (zum Beispiel *this year / week*), geschehen.	Das Treffen ereignete sich an einem bestimmten Ort zu einem Zeitpunkt der Vergangenheit.
4.	
I've *worked here* for two years.	I *worked there* for two years.
Die Situation, die in der Vergangenheit begonnen hat, dauert bis jetzt an.	Die Situation war von begrenzter Dauer und wurde in der Vergangenheit beendet.

Merlins Zwischenprüfung

A. Make your choice: Past Tense or Present Perfect.

1. Tramp: I *haven't eaten / didn't eat* for three days, mister.
   Ronny: My goodness! I wish I had your willpower.

6

2. Ronny: Do you really believe in free love?
   Anne: *Did I ever send / Have I ever sent* you a bill?

3. Graffiti:
   Professionals *have built / built* the Titanic.
   Amateurs *have built / built* the Ark.

B. Put the verbs in the brackets into the correct form.

1. Patient: Everybody hates me.
   Psychiatrist: Nonsense, you worm, you (*not meet*) everybody yet.

2. Bobby: You (*read*) the new Brockhaus Encyclopedia ?
   Ronny: No, I'm waiting for the film.

3. "Hey, barman, I (*order*) a pint. This glass is only three-quarters full."
   "Oh, that's a pint all right, sir. I just packed it in tightly."

C. Two mistakes in each example for you to correct.

1. Have you been to Egypt? I was there twice, but there were some
   things I haven't liked.

2. "How long have you stayed in Cairo?" I've been there for three
   years. Then I went on to Tunisia.

3. I always wanted to visit the pyramids. Now I found I can't stand the
   climate.

LEVEL II : Der feine Unterschied

6

Present Perfect	Past
5.	
I have seen him twice *since* he *has been* in Bonn. ... seit er in Bonn ist.	I haven't seen him *since* he *left* Bonn. ... seit er Bonn verlassen hat.
I've *worked here* for two years. ... seit zwei Jahren.	I *worked there* for two years. ... zwei Jahre lang.

✪ *Since* und *for* werden fälschlich oft als Signalwörter für Present Perfect angesehen. Sie lassen aber auch Past und Past Perfect zu.

Present Perfect	Past
6.	
We *haven't seen* Paul *today / this year.* Der Tag / das Jahr ist noch nicht vorüber.	We *didn't see* Paul *today / this year.* Der Tag ist vorüber. Der Satz wurde am Ende des Zeitraums gesagt.
7.	
I *haven't seen* Paul *recently.* ... in letzter Zeit.	I *saw* Paul *recently.* ... neulich, vor kurzem

✪ Einige Zeitangaben (*recently, just* ...) beziehungsweise Häufigkeitsadverbien ändern ihre Bedeutung je nach der gewählten Zeit.

Time for a SMILE

On a bus, an absent-minded professor *was looking* at the lady next to him and *exclaimed*, "Hello, Lydia Preston! I *haven't seen* you for ages. How you *have changed*! You *used to weigh* 75 kilos and now you are nothing but skin and bones. You *used to have* grey hair and now you are blond and ..." – "I beg your pardon," *interrupted* the lady, "I am not your Lydia Preston, my name is Johnson." – "Fancy that," *replied* the professor, "you *have changed* your name as well."

Merlins **Merlins Reifeprüfung**

D. Present Perfect or Simple Past?

1. Robert: I *have visited / visited* the Shetland Islands recently. There
were a lot of ponies around. Where have they gone?
Farmer: They drowned when we *tried / have tried* to train them for
surf riding.

6

2. Policeman: *Have you known / Did you know* that your wife fell out of
the car two or three kilometres ago?
Robert: Thank God for that, officer. I thought I had gone deaf.

3. I *have seen / saw* Bob at the railway station. He was with a pretty
blond girl.

E. Translate the German in the brackets.

1. What is an art critic?
Art critics are like eunuchs in a harem; they know how it's done, they
(*sehen*) it done every day, but they are unable to do it themselves.

2. Before the Socialists came to power we were on the edge of an
economic precipice.
Since then we (*nehmen*) a great step forward.

3. You (*hören*) about the Scot who won a holiday for two in Majorca?
He (*gehen*) by himself twice.

F. Put the words in brackets into the correct form.

1. Teacher to pupil:
"I never (*lie*) when I was a child."
"So when you (*start*), Sir?"

2. "How dare you belch in front of my family?"
"I'm sorry. I (*not know*) it was their turn."

Merlin's saga

6

Ron was walking along the main street of our pretty little university town, Heidelmountain. Suddenly he **saw** a *familiar shape* sitting on the steps of the church of the Holy Spirit. It **was** a depressed-looking Merlin. Ron **walked** over to him. "What **has happened** to you, old *wizard*? You look as if you have the *cares* of the world on your shoulders."

Merlin's sharp blue eyes **met** Ron's. "Cares of the world? Indeed I have." The lively Englishman continued *to probe.* "Recently, you **were** full of life, really motivated to help people with problems. What **has happened** since then?" Merlin leaned backed against the wall. "That's right. A few months ago I **felt** better. But since then I **have seen** *greed* and rudeness. Nobody is interested in or has love for his fellow men."

Ron wanted to be *supportive.* "Oh, that's not quite true. I'm sure it **was** the same some two thousand years ago." Merlin stood up. "No, young man. I **have been** around for many *centuries* and I **have never seen** such things. For example, young people here don't talk to each other. They prefer to speak into *cubes* of plastic which play metallic *tunes* to them. They have no time to stand and stare. They shoot past on pieces of wood with rollers on them. Laughing Ron interrupted. "Oh, you mean skateboards. "Maybe. In my youth we **had** horses." – "But it's only a matter of transport." Merlin was not happy.

"At least a horse **was** *alive.* That is not so with wood and plastic!"

vertraut; Gestalt

Zauberer
Sorgen

forschen
vor Kurzem

Habgier

hilfsbereit

Jahrhunderte

Würfel
Melodien

lebendig

Die Vorvergangenheit[1] – The Past Perfect

CHECK your Past Perfect

Spot the mistake

a. Just think, if Shakespeare had a computer, he probably would have accidentally erased *A Midsummer Night's Dream*.
b. Last night I dreamt I had invented a new type of breakfast food. When I woke up in the morning, I found that a corner of the mattress disappeared.
c. When she asked him why he has suddenly stopped loving her, he said he had a train to catch.

Tick them off

Right Wrong

a. When we arrived, she made tea.
b. When we arrived, she was already making tea.
c. When we arrived, she had already made tea.
d. When we had arrived, she made tea.
e. When we had arrived, she was making tea.
f. When we had arrived, she had made tea.

Time for a SMILE

Many years ago I chased a woman for almost two years, only to discover that her tastes were exactly like mine: we both were crazy about girls. (GROUCHO MARX)

---

1 Die Vorvergangenheit entspricht dem deutschen Plusquamperfekt.

Die Vorvergangenheit

Level I : Das Einmaleins des Past Perfect

Was ist das Past Perfect?

Nehmen wir zwei zeitlich aufeinander folgende Ereignisse A und B:

A: Peter left the room.   B: Paul entered.

Berichten wir in einem Satzgefüge (Haupt- und Nebensatz), muss klar sein, was vorher und was nachher geschah. Dafür sorgt das Zusammenspiel von *Past Perfect* und *Past Tense*.

Vorvergangenheit	Vergangenheit	Gegenwart	
B	**A**	**0**	Zeit

Peter *left* the room.   Paul *entered*.

Peter *had* already *left* the room (B), when Paul *entered* (A).

Das Past Perfect steht für

1. Ereignisse, die nicht in der zeitlichen Reihenfolge erzählt werden.
2. Situationen, die sich vor einem Zeitpunkt in der Vergangenheit ereigneten.

A man from Scotland *went* to Loch Ness alone on his honeymoon. – His wife *had been* there before.

The director *had never been* so upset as when Sue *asked* what he wanted to name the baby. Sue, that's his secretary.

Das Past Perfect Progressive[1] steht für

3. Handlungen, die bis zu einem Zeitpunkt der Vergangenheit andauerten. Betonung liegt auf deren Verlauf, nicht auf einem Resultat.

Last week we found that the woman *who'd been sitting watching* TV with us for the past eight years was a complete stranger. My wife thought she was my mother, and I thought she was hers.

1 Erinnerung: Nicht alle Verben können im Progressive stehen; siehe Seite 19.

Merlins **Merlins** Zwischenprüfung

A. **Which form is correct?**

1. An applicant who *had just completed / just completed* a series of multiple choice tests was asked by the teacher whether it pays to be honest. He immediately asked what the five alternatives were.

2. Judge: Now tell me, why did you steal that wallet?
   Prisoner: Your Honour, I *hadn't felt / hadn't been feeling* well on that day and I thought the change would do me good.

3. A happy event in church:
   After the priest *read / had read* the fourth commandment: "Thou Shalt Not Steal", I noticed my umbrella was gone. After he *read / had read* the seventh commandment: "Thou Shalt Not Commit Adultery", I suddenly *remembered / had remembered* where I had left it.

B. **Put the words in brackets into the correct form.**

1. "I could always tell when my girlfriend (*drink*). Her face would start getting blurred."

2. Bob: Last night I (*dream*) that I (*make love*) to the most beautiful girl in the world.
   Usch: And how (*be*) I?

3. "Doctor, Doctor, I've lost my memory."
   "When (*this / happen*)?"
   "When what (*happen*)?"

C. **Merlin's everyday problems.**

Put the verbs in brackets into the correct form.

Merlin _____ (*just come*) home from work when he _____ (*find*) a leak in his bathroom. Water _____ (*drip*) from the ceiling for some time, and there _____ (*be*) a large pool of water on the floor. As soon as he _____ (*see*) the leak, he _____ (*call*) the plumber. The plumber's wife _____ (*answer*): "I'm afraid he _____ (*go*) out an hour ago and he _____ (*not come*) back yet." Merlin _____ (*not expect*) an answer like that. "I'll have to get some magic together and do it that way," he moaned. (To be continued)

7

LEVEL II : Tipps für Kenner

7

4. Past Tense und Past Perfect im Vergleich

Past Tense	Past Perfect
I *started* tidying up the room *when* my sister *arrived*.	I *had started* tidying up the room *when* my sister *arrived*.
Aufeinander folgende Ereignisse: Ich begann ..., als sie ankam.	Ich hatte schon begonnen ..., als sie ankam.

5. Past Perfect Simple und Past Perfect Progressive im Vergleich

Past Perfect Simple	Past Perfect Progressive
I *had written* twelve offers by the time the boss arrived back.	I was tired. I *had been writing* offers for hours.
Die Betonung liegt auf dem Ergebnis der Tätigkeit.	Die Betonung liegt auf der Tätigkeit selbst und wie die Zeit verbracht wurde.

6. Spezialfälle

Manchmal verwenden native speakers Past Tense statt Past Perfect, wenn offensichtlich ist, was vorher und was nachher geschah. Dies ist oft in Sätzen mit *as soon as, after, before* und *when* der Fall.

Before the lights *went* out, Before the lights *had gone* out,	there was a big explosion.
As soon as I *heard* the explosion, As soon as I *had heard* the explosion,	I ran outside.
When I *opened* the window, When I *had opened* the window,	we heard cries for help.
Only after the police *arrived*, Only after the police *had arrived*,	could we leave the hotel.

Merlins Reifeprüfung

D. Create one sentence for each of the following pairs.

1. The plane landed.   I took my safety belt off.

2. I left the plane.   I noticed my luggage was missing.

3. I complained to the clerk.   I found my luggage lying on the floor.

E. Past Perfect or Past Perfect Progressive?

Which is more natural?

1. They *had driven / had been driving* for more than three hours when the trouble in the engine started.

2. Jenny *had gone / had been going* out with Bill for ten years before she heard about his double life.

3. As soon as I *had read / had been reading* the e-mail, I phoned the police.

4. Annette *had fallen / had been falling* asleep at least five times by the time the phone finally rang.

F. Merlin and the modern world (continued).

Put the verbs in the brackets into the correct form.

"I'll give them one more chance," thought Merlin. He _____ (*decide*) that after an hour or two's thought, because doing magic costs energy and he didn't have too much energy left after he _____ (*spend*) two days in that police cell. So he sat down to wait for the call. Two hours later the phone _____ (*ring*). "This is the plumber. You _____ (*call*) earlier." "Where on earth you _____ (*be*)?" demanded the wizard angrily.

"I _____ (*wait*) for two hours! What have you been doing all this time?" "I'm terribly sorry, sir. No sooner I _____ (*leave*) my house to come to you, than I had an accident. After the police _____ (*question*) me for more than an hour, they realised I wasn't drunk and let me go. That's why I'm late."

Merlin's saga

Bob, one of the *creators* of this masterpiece, went down to the riverside to meditate and think about the rest of his life. He **had been jogging** an hour before, so he was feeling very tired. He was sad. Actually Bob **had become** more and more *depressed* in the last few months. He wanted to try something new. He **had had** enough of this teaching game. "Your students just *draw* your energy out of you," Bob would *moan*. "If they have good results, it's because they are good. Bad results and it's the teacher's *fault*." Gradually Bob's eyes closed as he watched the water *drifting* past. He dreamed he could see the young *trout* flickering around in the water. Bob **had been dozing** for about an hour when he suddenly became aware that he was no longer alone. Poor old Bob **had got** a bit of a shock, but slowly he pulled himself together. Of course, it was our *ancient* hero, Merlin, who **had been** *peering* into his crystal ball when he came upon our sorry figure. "Oh," exclaimed Bob. "I **hadn't expected** to see you again." "Your negative vibrations *attracted* me," smiled the *weary* wizard. "You dream of a different life, walking through the forest, fishing for *salmon* in Canada, no *responsibilities*, no deadlines." Bob was stunned. Somehow the whitebeard **had** *read* his mind. That was exactly what **he had been thinking** about. Merlin spoke again. "Create a strategy, have a vision and put it into practice. Now sleep a little with the fish, and tomorrow your life will begin to change."	*Schöpfer*
	deprimiert
	ziehen
	wehklagen
	Schuld
	treiben
	Forelle
	uralt; spähen, gucken
	anziehen; müde, matt
	Lachs; Verantwortung
	Gedanken lesen

7

Über die Zukunft sprechen – Talking about the Future

CHECK Can you cope with the Future?

Which is the best choice?

a. If the weather is fine tomorrow,
  1. I am going to go for a jog.   **2.** I will go for a jog.

b. When we get home the kids
  1. will be sleeping.   **2.** will sleep.

c. When we get home
  1. I'll be going to bed immediately.   **2.** I'll go to bed immediately.

d. I am going to visit my mother as soon as
  1. I'll arrive in Berlin.   **2.** I arrive in Berlin.

e. When you read this picture postcard
  1. I'll be lying on the beach in Florida.   **2.** I'm going to lie on the beach in Florida.

f. Let me post this letter for you. On my way home
  1. I'll be passing the post office anyway.   **2.** I'll pass the post office anyway

✔ Tick them off

Right Wrong

a. Will you still be sending me Valentines when I'm sixty-four?

b. As soon as the German tourist will get to Paradise, he will ask for picture postcards.

c. Wait for me. I'll have finished this letter in a couple of minutes.

d. Tomorrow's cars are looking quite different.

55

Über die Zukunft sprechen

LEVEL I

Level I : Das Einmaleins der Zukunft

Vier Möglichkeiten, über die Zukunft zu sprechen	
1. Will-Future	
a. Voraussagen	Drinking *will not* stop your problems, but
b. Vermutungen	it *will give* you lots of interesting new ones.
c. Versprechen	Father: I *will give* a handsome prize to the man who marries my daughter.
	Young man: Can I see the prize first, Sir?
d. spontan gefasste Entschlüsse, Angebote und Reaktionen	A man was caught for speeding and had to go to court. "What will you take, 30 days or £300?" asked the judge. – "I think I'*ll take* the money," the man replied.
2. Going-to-Future	
a. Pläne, Vorhaben und Absichten	Voice on telephone: Give us $50,000 or you won't see your wife again.
	Scotsman: I'*m not going to* give you the money. But I'm interested in your offer.
b. Schlussfolgerung aufgrund vorhandener Anzeichen	Our son *is going to be* an auctioneer. This is the third valuable vase he has brought under the hammer.
3. Present Progressive*	
für persönlich arrangierte Situationen	"We'*re sending* our son to a holiday camp next week." – "Oh! Does he need a holiday?" – "No, but we do!"
4. Simple Present*	
für Situationen, die von einer höheren Autorität festgelegt sind oder die der Sprecher für nicht änderbar hält	"I *start* working at the Swan Laundry on Monday." – "Wonderful! But tell me, how do you wash a swan?"

* Damit es keine Verwechslung mit der Gegenwart gibt, muss der Zukunftsbezug aus Zeitangaben oder Kontext eindeutig hervorgehen.

Merlins *Merlins* Zwischenprüfung

A. Which of our Level I rules fits which sentence?

1. Doctor: I can't see anything wrong with you. It must be the alcohol.
   Ronald: Never mind. I'll come back when you're sober.

2. "What is your son going to be?"
   "A pensioner."

8

3. You have to admire my boss. If you don't, you don't work here any more.

Now look back at "Das Einmaleins der Zukunft" and decide which rule fits which sentence!

B. Which Future fits best?

1. Eat, drink and be happy – for tomorrow we _____
   a. will diet   **b.** diet   **c.** are going to diet

2. Ron: I _____ now. Don't trouble to show me to the door.
   Bob: It's no trouble. It's a pleasure.
   a. am going to go   **b.** go   **c.** will go

3. On the wall of an Oxford pub:
   Don't complain about the beer. You _____ old and weak yourself one day, too.
   a. 'll be being   **b.** 'll be   **c.** are

C. Put in the most appropriate Future form.

1. "Doctor, I'm afraid I (*die*)."
   "Nonsense, that's the last thing you'll do."

2. Fat Bessie Braddock to Winston Churchill:
   "Winston, you are drunk."
   "Bessie, you are ugly. But tomorrow I (*be*) sober."

3. He: Darling, if we get married do you think you (*be able*) to live on my income?
   She: Of course, darling, but what you (*live*) on?

LEVEL II : Tipps für Kenner

8

Will-Future Progressive

5. um auszudrücken, dass eine Situation zu einem Zeitpunkt (in einem Zeitraum) in der Zukunft gerade im Verlauf ist, das heißt sie *schon* begonnen hat und *noch nicht* beendet ist.

First fortune-teller: Lovely weather we're having, isn't it? Second fortune-teller: Yes, it reminds me of a fine summer day we'*ll be having* in 2040.

6. um auszudrücken, dass etwas sich "ohnehin", "sowieso", "zwangsläufig", "wie bereits geplant" oder weil es so üblich ist, ereignen wird.

We *will be landing* at Heathrow in 15 minutes.
You needn't send Paul a fax. You'*ll be meeting* him at the conference tomorrow, remember?

7. ferner zum Ausdruck einer höflichen Frage nach jemandes Plänen.

Will you be staying another night, sir?
Will you be paying cash or by credit card, sir?

Future Perfect Simple

8. für Situationen, die in der Zukunft abgeschlossen sein werden – meist mit Zeitangabe.

By the time you reach the age of 75 you'*ll have learnt* everything. All you have to do is to try and remember it.

Future Perfect Progressive

9. zur Betonung, dass eine zukünftige Handlung zu einem Zeitpunkt ununterbrochen im Gang sein wird – meist mit Zeitangabe.

By the time we are back home the kids *will have been watching* TV *for two hours.*

Merlins **Merlins Reifeprüfung**

D. What do the following sentences express?

1. She: Darling, *will you still love* me when I get old?

   He: Our love will grow stronger and stronger with each passing
        year. But you won't look like your mother, will you?

   a. spontane Reaktion   **b.** Bitte um   **c.** Bitte um
                                    Versprechen   Voraussage

2. "I'm not going to school anymore," shouted little Johnny back home
   after his first morning at school. "I can't read, I can't write,
   and *they won't let* me talk either."

   a. persönlich   **b.** Versprechen   **c.** Absicht,
        arrangierte Situation   Vorhaben

3. "This is a lovely district, isn't it? Wouldn't you like to come and
   spend a holiday here?"

   "Yes, *we'll be staying* in a place not far from here in the summer."

   a. Teil einer bereits   **b.** Absicht,   **c.** abgeschlossene
        geplanten Situation   Vorhaben   Situation in der
                                                              Zukunft

E. Choose the most appropriate form of the Future.

1. Client: I'd have to be an idiot to buy stock in your company.

   Tycoon: Well then, how many shares _____?

   a. are you going to buy   **b.** do you buy   **c.** will you buy

2. Bob: Have you got any plans for tonight?

   Ron: Yes, I _____ chess with my dog.

   Bob: It's amazing – it must be a really intelligent animal.

   Ron: Not really. I won three games to two last night.

   a. 'll be playing   **b.** 'll play   **c.** 'll have played

3. Tailor: Your suit _____ ready in six months, sir.

   Customer: Six months for a suit? Why, it only took six days to create
               the world.

   Tailor: Well, sir, but have you noticed the condition it is in?

   a. is going to be   **b.** is   **c.** will be

8

8

10. Weitere Ausdrucksmittel für künftiges Geschehen

be to für feste Vereinbarungen	Our Chancellor *is to meet* the French President in Paris next week.
be on the point of doing, *be about to do* für unmittelbar bevorstehende Ereignisse	The old bridge *is on the point of collapsing.* Nice to meet you, but we *are about to leave.*
be (un)likely/certain/sure, *be bound to do* zum Ausdruck der Sicherheit und Wahrscheinlichkeit	*It's likely to rain.* You've done so much work that you*'re bound to pass* the exam.
be expected, be supposed to do für etwas, das von jemandem in Zukunft erwartet wird; Zeitangabe ist notwendig	You*'re supposed to pay* the bill by Friday.

SPRACHFALLEN für Deutsche

Deutsch	Falsch	Englisch
Gehen Sie einkaufen?	*Will you go shopping now?*	*Will you be going* shopping?

✪ Einfaches Will-Future: Aufforderung – Verlaufsform: höfliche Bitte.

Deutsch	Falsch	Englisch
Wann kommst du zurück, Paul? Ich komme heim, wenn der Film aus ist.	*When do you come home, Paul?* *I come home when the film will be over.*	When will you be back home, Paul? I*'ll* be back when the film is over.

✪ Nach Fragewort (*when*) kann Will-Future stehen. Nach Konjunktionen (*when, as soon as, by the time*) steht in Zeit-Nebensätzen die einfache Gegenwart.

Deutsch	Falsch	Englisch
Wenn er mich fragen wird, werde ich nein sagen.	*If he will ask me, I will say 'no'.*	If he *asks* me, I will say 'no'.

✪ In Bedingungssätzen steht im Nebensatz mit *if* (meist) kein *will*.

Merlin's Merlin's saga

Living in the future is sometimes not so easy for an old *wizard* like Merlin. He had discussed this problem with a young *witch* two or three thousand years before. "I know I **will have to** adapt to certain things," he mumbled. The witch *cackled.* "You'**ll have had** enough of those modern men after a week or two. You'**ll be wishing** you were back with us, the real people." Well, she was certainly right. Anyway, Merlin decided to adapt to the new *environment.* "Instead of using and wasting my valuable magic, I'**ll pick up** a few of their modern ways." And so it came to pass that we see the old whitebeard sitting in front of a "*pinstripe suit*" at the Drednet Bank. Merlin and the pinstripe are somehow centuries apart. We'**ll just listen** in on their conversation for a few minutes.

"So, I'**ll certainly need** to *borrow* some money from you to make my stay in this century more effective."

"Well, you'**ll have** to fill out these twenty-five forms first. And I'll need *proof* of your *earnings.* How much **will you** be *applying* **for**? And what **are you going to do** with the money?"

"What **will you ask** next? That is my business, young sir."

"These are standard questions, Mr Merlin. We **are bound to** check out what you'**ll be using** the money for."

"Young man, I **leave** this century at quarter to midnight and I expect an answer or you **will wish** you had never seen me."

Zauberer
Hexe

8

gackern

Umwelt
annehmen

Nadelstreifen-
anzug

leihen

Nachweis; Ein-
künfte; beantra-
gen

Indirekte Rede – Indirect Speech

CHECK your Indirect Speech

 Spot the mistake

a. Tina thought Robinson Crusoe is a world famous tenor.

b. The first time the little girl from the big city ever saw a cow she thought it was a bull that has swallowed a glove.

c. Have you heard about the Irish explorer who paid £10 for a sheet of sandpaper? – He thought it's a map of the Sahara Desert.

d. An Irish professor announced that he has performed his first appendix transplant.

Tick them off **Right** **Wrong**

a. "An alcoholic," my doctor told me, "is a person who drinks more than his doctor."

b. I told my psychiatrist that I didn't believe in reincarnation last time, either.

c. Tim told his teacher he was so poor, he can't even pay attention.

d. He whispered into my ear that the new accountant has all the characteristics of a dog – except loyalty.

e. Sometimes I think that God, in creating man, somewhat overestimated his ability. (OSCAR WILDE)

Time for a SMILE

His mother *told him* that eating plenty of spinach *would* put colour in his cheeks. And it did. He's the only kid in the street with green cheeks.

LEVEL I : Das Einmaleins der indirekten Rede

1. Was ist indirekte Rede?

In der indirekten Rede wird berichtet, was jemand gesagt, geschrieben, gedacht, geträumt, gefragt oder befohlen hat. Sie wird eingeleitet durch einen Einleitungssatz mit einem Verb, das die jeweilige Sprechabsicht deutlich macht.

9

Aussage	Frage	Aufforderung
agree, answer, advise, feel, point out, say, think	*ask, want to know, enquire, wonder*	*invite, suggest, tell, ask* (bitten), *order*

Folgendes Beispiel enthält alle drei Formen:

	So wurde es gesagt	So wird es berichtet
Aussage	Patient: Doctor, I often feel like killing myself.	A patient *tells* his doctor (that) he often *feels* like killing himself and he *asks* him *what to do.*
Frage	What shall I do?	
Aufforderung	Doctor: Just leave that problem to me.	The doctor *tells* the man *to* leave that problem to him.

2. Indirekte Aussage ohne Änderung der Zeiten

Ist der Einleitungssatz im Present, Present Perfect oder Future, bleiben die Zeiten der direkten Rede in der indirekten Rede erhalten.

Einleitungssatz

Present	A pessimist is a man who *thinks* (that) all women *are* bad. An optimist hopes so.
Present Perfect	Father to Peggy: Mother *has told* me that you *are* pregnant. But are you sure it's yours?
Future	A statistician is a person who, if you've got your feet in the oven and your head in the refrigerator, *will tell you* that, on average, you *are* very comfortable.

Indirekte Rede

3. Indirekte Aussage und *backshift*

Steht der Einleitungssatz in einer Zeit der Vergangenheit, verschieben sich die Zeiten jeweils in die nächst fernere Vergangenheit (*backshift*). Ausnahme: Konditional und Past Perfect werden nicht verändert.

Direkte Rede		Indirekte Rede
a. I *feel* happy, said Bob.		Bob said he *felt* happy.
Simple Present	→	**Simple Past**
b. And you'*re looking* happy, agreed Tina.		Tina agreed that he *was looking* happy.
Present Progressive	→	**Past Progressive**
c. I'm happy and lucky because I *won* £10,000 at the horse races yesterday, explained Bob.		Bob explained that he was happy and lucky because he *had won* £10,000 at the horse races the day before.
Simple Past	→	**Past Perfect**
d. At the horse races! And I *was looking* for you everywhere, remarked Tina.		Tina remarked a bit angrily that she *had been looking* everywhere for Bob.
Past Progressive	→	**Past Perfect Progressive**
e. Ten thousand pounds! It's the first time we'*ve* ever *won* anything, Bob exclaimed.		Bob exclaimed that it was the first time they *had* ever *won* anything.
Present Perfect Simple	→	**Past Perfect**
f. We *have been waiting* for years to win something, haven't we? added Bob.		And he added that they *had been waiting* for years to win something.
Present Perfect Progressive	→	**Past Perfect Progressive**
g. From now on I'*ll try* my luck again and again, said Bob.		Bob said from that day on he *would try* his luck again and again.
will	→	**would**

Merlins Zwischenprüfung

A. What did they actually say?

1. Anne told Henrietta that she would be glad when they had eaten the last of the rhinoceros.

2. Tim said that nothing that was worth knowing could be taught.

9

3. Bob moaned that his petrol tank had sprung a leak.

B. Make your choice.

1. "I'm informed from many quarters that a rumour *had / has* been put about that I died this morning. This is quite untrue."
   (Winston Churchill)

2. And then there was the Irish helicopter pilot who crashed. He thought that it *is /was* too cold so he turned the fan off.

3. Eve was the most frustrated of women: she couldn't nag Adam by telling him what a wonderful man her first husband *is / was.*

C. Put the following into indirect speech.

Beginnen Sie mit einem Einleitungssatz in der Vergangenheit.

1. Bob: A genius (*is*) anybody who could describe how an accordion (*works*) without using his hands.

2. Ron: Which book do you like best?
   Anne: I (*like*) my husband's chequebook most.

3. G. B. Shaw: Old age (*is*) not so bad when you (*consider*) the alternative.

4. Ron: I'll be driving to Spain in summer.

LEVEL II : **Tipps für Fortgeschrittene**

9

---

4. Kein *backshift* bei aktuellem Sachverhalt

Eine Rückverschiebung der Zeiten ist nicht immer sinnvoll. In folgenden Fällen *kann* sie unterbleiben:

a. Die Mitteilung trifft zur Zeit der Berichterstattung noch zu oder sie steht noch bevor.

Let's hurry, Tom. In the news they *warned* that the hurricane *is / was* rapidly moving from the Pacific towards Miami Beach.

b. Die Aussage erhebt Anspruch auf Allgemeingültigkeit, weil sie Gewohnheit, Eigenschaft oder Naturgesetz ist.

Matti said that in Finland, where he *comes* from, the sun doesn't *rise* in winter at all.

---

5. Keine Veränderung mancher modaler Hilfsverben

a. Die meisten modalen Hilfsverben (*need, would, could, might, should, ought to, used to, would like to, had better*) werden nicht verändert. Bei *must* gibt es zwei Möglichkeiten.

She said she must go / had to go.

b. Wir merken uns: Nur *can, may, must, will, shall* werden verändert.

Direkte Rede	Indirekte Rede
Any fool *can* make a rule.	A wise man *said* that any fool *could* make a rule.
Time *may* be a great healer, but it's a lousy beautician.	Time *might* be a great healer, but it is a lousy beautician, *sighed* the aging film star.
Nobody *will* ever invade Germany. Who can afford to live here?	Tom *said* that nobody *would* ever invade Germany. Who could afford to live there?
Democracy ensures that we *shall* be governed no better than we deserve. (G. B. SHAW)	Shaw *said* Democracy *ensured* that we *should be* governed no better than we deserve.

9

6. Sprechabsichten und Gefühle

a. Es erfordert Fingerspitzengefühl, die Sprechabsichten zu erkennen und zu berichten. Hier einige einleitende Verben: *agree, answer, advise, exclaim, explain, feel, greet, hope, offer, point out, protest, suggest.*

Why don't we go to the cinema?	He *suggested* going to the cinema.
What about a drink?	She *offered* me a drink.
You'd better leave at once.	He *advised* me to leave at once.

b. Die Übermittlung von Ausrufen und emotionalen Fragmenten ist schwierig und oft nicht erforderlich (zum Beispiel *question tags*).

Hello! What do you want?	He *greeted* me and asked what I wanted.
Good Lord! It's impossible.	He was totally *amazed.*
Oh! I've burned myself.	She *cried out* that she had burned herself.
Let's help them, shall we?	He *suggested* that we should help them.

7. Weitere Veränderungen

✪ Verändert werden Ortsangaben, wenn der Berichtende sich an einem anderen Ort befindet als seine Quelle.
✪ Verändert werden Zeitangaben, wenn direkte Rede und Bericht nicht innerhalb desselben Zeitraums liegen und
✪ Pronomen, wenn der Berichtende nicht von sich selbst spricht.

	So wird es gesagt	**So wird berichtet**
Ortsangaben	here	there
	in this country	in Britain
Zeitangaben	now	then
	today, tonight	that day, that night
	tomorrow	the following day
	yesterday	the day before
	an hour / day ago	an hour / day before
Pronomen	this	that
	I, you, we,	he, she, they
	my, your	his, her
	our, your	their

Merlins **Reifeprüfung**

D. Translate the verbs in brackets into the correct form.

1. When a Texas school class was told that next day they (*lernen*) to draw, eighteen boys turned up with pistols.

9

2. Bob told Ron that he (*nicht glauben können*) a word he was saying, so he certainly couldn't believe any of Ron's sentences.

3. Ron's old stories about himself: he was telling us that he only (*brauchen*) four minutes to run a mile.

E. Spot the mistake.

1. Ron said that he doesn't need to answer the question.

2. Sue said she may be late.

3. Salesman: Sir, my wife said I shall ask for a raise.
   Sales Manager: I'll ask my wife if I might give you one.

F. Put the sentences into Indirect Speech.

1. "What about having a short holiday?"

2. "Would you like to use my car?"

3. "No, I can't accept that at all."

4. "Watch what you're doing!"

Merlin's saga

Living in Germania is not easy. Merlin soon realised that he **could** not simply **run** around *doing magic* and good things. Bob **warned** him not **to practise** magic as a *freelancer*. "You could get problems with our special *pseudo-self-employment* laws," smiled Bob. Merlin replied **that he thought** that **was** a very long word. "Not nearly as long and complicated as the law itself", laughed Bob. Merlin was not amused. He wanted to know what he should do about it. Bob **told him to go** to the *"office"*. He **advised him to get** the information there.

zaubern
Freiberufler
Scheinselbständig-keitsgesetz

Amt

Off went the sage to the *trading office*. They **told him he should** sit outside and wait his turn. Merlin waited and waited. After an hour he was sitting in front of a *cross-looking* fellow who was more interested in eating his sandwich than talking to this *old fellow*. "So you want to practise magic. Well, you'll need a special *permit* for that." Merlin **couldn't believe what he was hearing**. He **informed** the young fellow **that he had been doing** magic for centuries. "I'm a first-class wizard, I have been for more than a thousand years." The *clerk* **made it clear** to Merlin that he *didn't care* **if he was** the Lord of the Rings himself. "If you want to do this job here you must have learned the *profession* here. You must show your exam certificates." Merlin's white beard began to turn red. That was the last thing the clerk noticed as he became smaller and smaller. He heard Merlin's voice booming loud. "I **warned you that you would have** to accept my qualifications. They're original, you know."

Gewerbeamt

mürrisch drein-blickend
alter Knabe
Zulassung

Sachbearbeiter
egal sein

Beruf

Indirekte Fragen und Anweisungen – Indirect Questions and Instructions

CHECK Check your Indirect Speech

Spot the mistake

a. If someone asks me what is two and two, I answer "Are you buying or selling?"
b. He asked her bring me the book.
c. The electrician complained that people asked him come and repair the bell and then didn't open the door.

Tick them off

Right Wrong

a. "I'd like to know how long can a human being live without a brain." – "Well, how old are you?"
b. Do you know what is the difference between a chess player and a civil servant? ... Well, a chess player moves every now and then.
c. He asked me if I knew who the new supermarket is?

Time for a SMILE

A rich banker who had made a fortune on the stock exchange phoned his new mistress:
"Darling, I sent you a birthday present: a Picasso and a Ferrari. Did you get them alright?"
"Yes darling, they are wonderful. But *could you* please *tell me which* is the Picasso and *which* is the Ferrari?"

Level I : Das Einmaleins der indirekten Fragen und Anweisungen

Indirekte Fragen

Einleitende Verben: *ask, want to know, enquire, wonder ...*

Direkte Frage	Indirekte Frage
1. *"What's* your name and *where* do you live?" she asked me.	She asked me *what* my name was and *where* I lived.

○ Fragewörter *who, where, which, how* etc. werden wiederholt.

2. "Are you married?" she wanted to know.	Then she wanted to know *if* (*whether*) I was married.

○ Ist kein Fragewort vorgegeben, steht *if* oder *whether* (ob).

3. "Where is Tom?" asked Sue.	Sue asked where Tom was.

○ Die Wortstellung ist (anders als im Deutschen) wie im Aussagesatz: Subjekt – Verb – Objekt

4. What must I do? Where shall I put it?	She asked me *what to do / where to put* it.

○ Anweisungen holt man so ein: Fragewort + Infinitiv mit *to*

○ Für Zeitverschiebung und Anpassung von Pronomen, Orts- und Zeitangaben gelten die Regeln der indirekten Rede.

Time for a SMILE

The Personnel Manager *asked* the applicant *if* she could write shorthand. "Yes," was her reply, "but it takes me longer."

Asked what he thought about Heaven and Hell, Mark Twain replied he didn't want to express an opinion, because he had friends in both places.

Indirekte Fragen und Anweisungen

10

Indirekte Anweisungen

Einleitende Verben: *advise, ask* (bitten)*, command, instruct, invite, suggest, tell, order, warn*

✪ Indirekte Befehle, Ratschläge, Einladungen, Bitten werden oft durch *to* + Infinitiv (verneint *not to*) wiedergegeben.

Direkte Aufforderung	→ Indirekte Aufforderung
5. Mother to Tom: Tommy, *come back*, at once. *Don't touch* this dog again.	His mother *told* Tom *to come* back at once and *not to touch* that dog again.
6. *You'd better* be careful with stray dogs.	She *advised* Tom *to be* careful with stray dogs.
7. *Won't you have* some ice-cream, Tom?	She *invited* Tom *to have* some ice-cream.
8. *Please* take Dad some ice-cream, too.	She *asked* Tom *to take* his father some ice-cream, too.

Time for a SMILE

A priest and an Austrian with an enormous dog were sitting in a railway compartment. The priest asked politely *what sort of dog it was*. "It's a cross between a priest and an ape," said the Austrian. "I see, then it is related to both of us," was the clever reply.

Indirect Questions and Instructions

Merlins Zwischenprüfung

A. What did they actually say?

1. The teacher informed the pupils that on that day they were trying to do without their calculators. She asked what 3 x 7 was. A pupil wanted to know when they were to hand in the results.

2. He asked why George was a born executive. She answered that his father owned the business.

3. Ron asked Bob how you doubled the price of a Trabi. Bob told him to fill up the petrol tank.

B. Report what they said.

1. Bob: I don't like tongue in wine sauce. The idea of eating something that has been in a cow's mouth disgusts me.
   Ron: Do you eat eggs then?

2. Bob: Alcoholics Anonymous? Isn't it a place where whisky is drunk in secret?

3. Sign in the undertaker's window: Drive carefully – we can wait.

C. Convert the following sentences into Indirect Speech.

1. "You should check that out before you spend the money."

2. "Will you join me on my trip to Egypt?"

3. "Please be careful what you say to Helen. She's very sensitive."

4. Boss to secretary: "If Mr. Walker calls before I return, tell him to call again at 5 o'clock."– "Okay, boss, but what shall I tell him if he doesn't call?"

LEVEL II : Tipps für Kenner

10

Direkte Frage ➜	Indirekte Frage
9. Who called while I was out? Did she leave a message?	He asked *who* had called and *if* he had left a message.

✪ Fragenketten werden mit *and* verbunden.

a. Is the window open? It's cold.	He said it was cold, *and asked if* the window was open.
b. May I have an apple? They look nice.	He asked if he might have an apple, *as* they looked nice.

✪ a. Bei Kombination von Frage und Aussage muss jeder Redeteil mit einem passenden Verb eingeleitet werden.

✪ b. Stellt man die Frage voran, kann man die Aussage mit einer geeigneten Konjunktion anschließen.

10. "Will you marry me?" – "No / Yes."	He *asked* me *if* I would marry him, and *I said I would / wouldn't.*
"Do you love me?" – "Yes / No."	He *asked* me if I loved him *and I replied I did / didn't.*

✪ Kombiniert man Fragen und kurze Yes- / No-Antworten, muss die indirekte Antwort mit einem Verb eingeleitet und ergänzt werden (zum Beispiel mit *would / wouldn't; did / didn't*).

Direkte Aufforderung ➜	Indirekte Aufforderung
11. Wait there till I call, *will you*?	I asked him to wait till I called him.

✪ *Question tags* fallen weg.

12. Don't spend all your money on clothes. Save something for the future.	I told him not to spend all his money on clothes *but to* save something for the future.

✪ Zwei Imperative können durch eine passende Konjunktion verbunden werden.

SPRACHFALLEN für Deutsche

	Falsch	Richtig
Er sagte, er sei krank.	*He said he is ill.*	He said he *was* ill.
Sie fragte mich, wo Tom sei (ist).	*She asked me where was Tom.*	She asked me where Tom *was*.

10

Direkte Frage ➜ **Indirekte Frage**

What about a drink?	*She said what about a drink.*	She *offered* me a drink.
Oh! I've burned myself.	*She cried 'oh' and that she had burned herself.*	She *cried out* that she had burned herself.
Good Lord! It's impossible.	*He said Good Lord and that it was impossible.*	He *exclaimed* that it was impossible.

Time for a SMILE

The life insurance agent thought that his son was marrying into a rather dodgy family, but quite how dodgy he didn't realise until the wedding when he announced that he was going to give his boy a free life insurance policy.

"Oh, no!" screamed the bride. "Don't do it! I don't want Daddy to set him on fire like he did the warehouse."

Merlins Reifeprüfung

D. Put the following sentences into Indirect Speech.

1. Worried young girl: Doctor, this new diet you've put me on makes me feel so passionate and sexy that I got carried away last night and bit off my boyfriend's ear.
   Doctor: Don't worry, it's only forty to fifty calories.

2. During the war two German spies were in a pub in London. They didn't want to be recognised as Germans so one of them ordered in English.
   "May I have two martinis, please!"
   "Dry?" asked the barman.
   "No," said the German. "Zwei!"

3. Slogan on a mechanic's T-shirt: Don't ask me; I was hired for my looks.

E. What did they really say?

1. Bob offered me a chance to go walking with him in the Black Forest.

2. Ron expressed his shock and disbelief in the German system.

3. She cried out when she dropped the plate.

F. Spot the mistake.

1. An elderly lady entered a pet shop and said to the shop assistant that she is disappointed with the canary she had been sold. She complained that it is lame. The shop assistant asked her whether she wants a singer or a dancer.

2. Short-sighted old Bob browsing in the antique shop: He asked the shop assistant what that old figure is worth and she replied it is worth about £200,000, but that it's the owner.

Merlin's saga

Ron wanted to go back for a short holiday to his country of origin across the Channel. He asked Merlin **if he wanted to go** with him for a *short break*. Ron **advised the wizard to go** since Merlin always looked *pale* and tired. The ancient fellow **agreed to accept** the *invitation* and off they went.

Kurzurlaub
blass
Einladung

The two friends travelled along rapidly in Ron's big, black Swedish-steel car and soon they reached the sea. The people at the ticket control **asked the travellers to drive** on board the ferry. They had been at sea about half an hour when suddenly a storm *brewed up*. Merlin was not used to this sort of weather. He'd also never been on a ship. "I feel a bit strange in my *stomach*. It must be hunger." Ron *recommended* **that Merlin ate** something. Off *staggered* the whitebeard and found a bar. He **asked if he could** have something to eat. "I'm sorry, mate," said the barman. "We don't have food here. Only this Toblerone." It was a huge *triangular* block of chocolate. Merlin paid the money and sat down to eat his meal. In a few minutes he had *polished off* the whole bar. The wizard went up to the deck for some fresh air. It was still windy, but the storm had passed. His head began to spin, the sea went up and down. Merlin's stomach went up and down, too. Then he was sick over the *railings* into the sea. Ron saw what had happened. He ran over to Merlin and **asked him what he had eaten**. Merlin, whose face was green, described the Toblerone. Ron **shouted at Merlin that he should** have eaten something sensible and healthy, to which Merlin replied by *throwing up* over the rails again. The *bottom line*: don't eat Swiss chocolate on an empty stomach in bad weather.

sich zusammen-brauen
Magen
empfehlen; taumeln

dreieckig

wegputzen

Reling

sich übergeben
Fazit

Aktiv und Passiv – Active and Passive

CHECK your Actives and Passives

 Spot the mistake

a. This money was promised to me from Dr Bossy.
b. The poor chap was killed by a knife.
c. Turn on the radio. An interesting programme is broadcast at the moment.
d. About this scandal was spoken again and again.
e. Grandma Mary enjoys to be told about our plans.

 Tick them off   **Right Wrong**

a. An egg is something that is never beaten when it is bad.
b. Tom is considered the best salesman. He can sell refrigerators to Eskimos.
c. Abstinence is a good thing, but it should be practised in moderation.
d. I'm living so far beyond my income that we may almost be said to be living apart. (E. E. CUMMINGS)
e. I don't believe you. This photo can't be taken in Japan.

Time for a SMILE

The bearded man stuck a gun in the pilot's back and hissed
"I want *to be taken* to London!"
"But *we're supposed to be going* to London anyway."
"I know. But I've been hijacked to Cuba twice before, so this time
 I'm taking no chances!"

Level I : Das Einmaleins des Passivs

- ✪ Aktiv und Passiv sind verschiedene Sichtweisen einer Situation.
- ✪ Der Aktivsatz betont, wer Täter oder was Ursache der Handlung ist. Beide sind Subjekt des Aktivsatzes.
- ✪ Der Passivsatz hingegen betont die Person oder Sache, mit der etwas geschieht. Sie ist Subjekt des Passivsatzes.

11

	Subjekt	Verb	Objekt
Activ	Mr Bucker	*helped*	James
Passiv	James	*was helped*	by Mr Bucker

Der Täter bleibt oft unerwähnt, weil unwichtig, unbekannt oder vorher erwähnt. Soll er im Satz erscheinen, wird er mit *by* angehängt.

Bildung der Zeiten

✪ Man nehme eine Form von *be* + Partizip Perfekt.

Infinitive	Monogamy leaves a lot to be desired.
Simple Present	A man who steals a horse *is put* into prison; a man who steals a whole country *is made* king.
Present Progressive	All the things I used to do when I was a kid are now *being done* by batteries.
Simple Past	High heels *were invented by a woman* who didn't like to be kissed on her forehead.
Past Progressive	He has bad reflexes. He was once run over by a car that *was being pushed* by two guys.
Present Perfect* **Past Perfect***	A pessimist is a man who *has been* forced to live with an optimist. America *had* often *been discovered* before Columbus, but it had always been hushed up.
Will-future	The longer one saves something before throwing it away, the sooner it *will be needed* after it is thrown away.

*Diese Zeiten haben kein Progressive im Passiv.

Merlins Zwischenprüfung

11

A. Identify the Passives.

1. Doctor: Miss Smith, you have acute appendicitis.
   Miss Smith: Doctor, I came here to be examined, not to be admired.

2. An executive is a man who hires others to do what he is hired to do.

3. They had drunk the bottle of wine before we arrived.

B. Convert Active into Passive and vice versa.

1. Jenny, somebody wants you on the phone.
2. They sell our books more cheaply in Russia.
3. Let's hope we can persuade them not to cancel the order.
4. We will offer them special conditions.

   Now put the following into the Active Voice.
5. If you see a gun fight, get into it so you won't be shotas a bystander.
6. High heels are worn by a woman who no longer wants to be kissed on her forehead.

C. Build Passive sentences.

1. The Watergate Principle:
   Government corruption / always report / in the past tense.
   Murphy's Laws

2. Bachelors know more about women than married men do.
   If they didn't, *they / marry / too.*

3. "Will you kiss me?"
   "But I've got scruples."
   "That's alright. *I / be / vaccinate.* "

LEVEL II

LEVEL II : Tipps für Kenner

1. Im Englischen gibt es mehr Verben, die ein Passiv bilden können, als im Deutschen.	The best advice Tom was ever *given* was when his father said, "Son, here's a million dollars. Don't lose it." Ebenso bei: *help, assist, follow, thank*
2. Die Verben des Sagens und Denkens bilden ein persönliches Passiv + Infinitiv mit *to*. Deutsch meist "sollen, angeblich"	What a salesman! He *is said* to be able to sell ice cubes to the Eskimos.
3. Die Partikel (Präpositionen, Adverbien) der *phrasal verbs* stehen nach dem Verb.	When you dance with Ron you feel as if you are being danced *against* rather than danced *with*. Ebenso bei: *ask for, look for, laugh at, put up with, think of, talk about* etc.
4. Verben mit zwei Objekten: meist wird die Person zum Subjekt des Passivsatzes.	*Tom* was given a million by his father. statt: *A million* was given *to* Tom ... Ebenso bei: *ask, offer, promise, send*
5. Steht im Aktiv ein Gerund, steht es auch im Passivsatz.	When I do something without *being told*, I'm trying to be smart. When my boss does the same, that's initiative.
6. In der Umgangssprache steht oft das Passiv mit *get* (nur für Handlungen).	Most people work just hard enough not to *get fired*, and *get paid* just enough money not to quit.

SPRACHFALLEN  für Deutsche

	Falsch	Richtig
The pub *was* already *closed* when we arrived.	wurde geschlossen	*war* geschlossen
The pub *will be closed* by the police.	wird geschlossen	*wird* geschlossen *werden*
He *is known* to be a thief.	Er ist bekannt als Dieb.	*Es ist bekannt*, dass er ein Dieb ist.

Merlins Reifeprüfung

11

D. Build Passive sentences.

1. If man had been meant to fly he (*be born*) with wings.

2. For every person wishing to teach there are thirty persons who (*not want / teach*).

3. Mary is the best housekeeper in the world. She (*divorce*) by fifteen husbands – and she's kept all the fifteen houses.

E. Change into the Passive.

Instructions at the company:

1. Staff members must accompany their visitors at all times.
   Visitors must _____.

2. Don't remove the handbooks from the copiers.

3. You can borrow mobiles on request.

F. Put in the correct Passive forms.

1. Bob: When I was seven years old I (*take*) to London Zoo.
   Ron: Were you (*accept*)?

2. Read in a newspaper: Prince Philip flew into London Airport last night. It (*hope*) that it (*rebuild*) by the end of the week.

3. If paintings can (*forge*) well enough to fool experts, why is the original so valuable? (GEORGE CARLIN)

Merlin's saga

Bob **was depressed** again. He had decided his health *left* a lot *to be desired.* He felt **worn out**.

zu wünschen übrig lassen;

"I'll **get** myself **checked**," he said to himself. And that is exactly what he did. Three days of tests at the local hospital. "Can I have my results?" Bob was *disappointed*. "You **will be informed** in two weeks, and not a day earlier."

ausgelaugt enttäuscht

11

Bob *limped* off to his sports club where he quickly ran two kilometres. Then he **was** suddenly **stopped** by a sharp pain in his Achilles *tendon*. "That **was programmed** to happen," he *wimpered*.

hinken

Sehne jammern

Bob was sitting at the side of the track feeling sorry for himself. He lay back and stared at the sky into the green trees. And there was our hero, the white and *weary* wizard, sitting on a branch. "Your money **was wasted**, going to those doctors. You **would be** better **advised** to try natural cures."

müde

Bob **felt attacked**. "No, I **was told** to go and **get** myself **checked** immediately." The wizard smiled *knowingly*. "And what exactly **was done** by those so-called doctors?"

wissend

"Well, my *liver* **was checked**, my lungs, my heart and many other bits and pieces."

Leber

Merlin looked at Bob. "And **have** you **been helped** by all these machines and specialists?" "Yes, I feel better, more *secure*." "Exactly," *hissed* the wizard. "Your illness is hidden somewhere in your *soul*, not in your body. **Be warned**!"

sicher; zischen Seele

Modale Hilfsverben – Modal Auxiliaries

CHECK your Modals

 ### Spot the mistake

a. I mustn't tell my wife anything. My neighbours do it for me.

b. Tom is a genius. He can everything. He can even Chinese.

c. "Doctor! Whenever I try to drink tea my eye hurts. What will I do?" – "Hmmm! Try taking the spoon out of the glass!"

 ### Tick them off

Right Wrong

a. An Italian prime minister *ought not to* think of getting married until he gets a steady job.

b. A pub advertises: "Our steaks are so tender that we don't know how that cow *might* walk."

c. "Daddy," said the bright child accompanying her father on a round of golf. "Why *mustn't* the ball go into the little hole?"

d. It's the final proof of God's omnipotence that he *couldn't* exist in order to save us.

Time for a SMILE

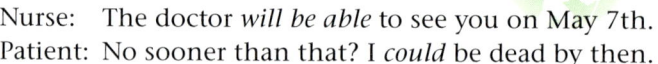

Nurse: The doctor *will be able* to see you on May 7th.
Patient: No sooner than that? I *could* be dead by then.
Nurse: Never mind, you *can* always cancel your appointment.

Level I : Das Einmaleins der Modalen Hilfsverben

Modal Auxiliaries (kurz *Modals*) ändern die Bedeutung eines Satzes.
Sie drücken aus, was geschehen *kann, darf, soll, sollte, muss.*

Überblick

	Bejaht	Verneint
Er kann	He can	He cannot / He can't
Er konnte / Er könnte	He could	He could not / He couldn't
Er darf	He may	He may not /
		He must not / He mustn't
Er dürfte	He might	He might not / He mightn't
Er will / Er wird	He will / He'll	He will not / He won't
Er würde / Er wollte	He would / He'd	He would not / He wouldn't
Er muss	He must	He need not / He needn't
Er sollte	He should	He should not / He shouldn't
Er sollte eigentlich	He ought to	He ought not / He oughtn't
Ich soll / Ich werde	I shall	I shall not / I shan't

Modals sind anders

	Vollverb	Modals
a. **Dritte Person Singular:** im Simple Present kein *-s*	He work*s*.	He *can* work.
b. **Frage und Verneinung:** keine Umschreibung mit *do*	*Does* he work? He *doesn't* work.	*May* he work? He *mustn't* work.
c. **Frageanhängsel:** Wiederaufnahme des *Modals*	He works here, *doesn't* he?	He can work here, *can't* he?
d. **Ersatzformen** im Past, Perfect, Future (siehe Seite 87)	He *has* never *worked*.	He *has* never *had to* work.

Modale Hilfsverben

12

Was drücken die Modals aus?

1. can / could

a. Fähigkeit / Unfähigkeit	Automatic is everything you *can't* repair yourself. They had pollution in the old days, too, but at least you *could* put it on your roses.
b. Erlaubnis / Verbot	Mum, now that I'm sixteen, *can I wear* short skirts and put on make-up? – No, John, *you can't*!
c. Möglichkeit / Unmöglich-keit	Elephants *can* have fleas, but fleas *can't* have elephants. When I was a boy I was told that anybody *could* become Chancellor. I'm beginning to believe it.

2. may / might

a. Höfliche Bitte	Customer: *May* I have a pair of alligator shoes? Salesman: Certainly! What size is your alligator?
b. Möglichkeit, Vermutung	He *may* drink to forget, but he never forgets to drink. Conscience is the inner voice which warns us that someone *might* be looking.

3. will / would

a. Bitte, Wunsch	The Telecom hotline received a call from an elderly lady: "My telephone cord is too long. *Will* you please pull it back at your end?"
b. Anordnung, Befehl	Judge: You *will* tell the truth, the whole truth, and nothing but the truth. Accused: With limitations like that, I don't think I have anything to say.
c. Angebot, Einladung	"*Would* you like a lemon with your tea?" – "No. I prefer to be alone."
d. Typisches Verhalten	The typical German tourist: As soon he gets to Paradise, he *will* ask for picture-postcards.

12

4. must	
a. Zwang, Notwendigkeit	"Do you serve women in this bar?" "No, sir, you *must* bring your own."
b. Rat, Vorschlag oft mit *simply, really*	If you like laws and sausages, you *must not* watch either of them being made. (OTTO VON BISMARCK)
c. Schlussfolgerung, Gewissheit	Did you see those pictures of the moon? They *must* have the same gardener we have.
d. Anordnung, Befehl	Rabbi: You *must* forgive your enemies and repay all your debts. David: Rabbi, I asked you here for spiritual help and you're talking business.

5. shall / should / ought to	
a. Bitte um Anweisung (mit *I / we*)	"What *shall* I give my wife for Christmas?" "Well, ask her what she wants." "No, no, I don't want to spend that much."
b. Ratschlag	You *should / ought* to go to a dentist and have some wisdom teeth put in.
c. Verpflichtung	Employer: You *should / ought* to have been here at nine o'clock. Employee: Why, what happened?

6. Einige Modals haben Ersatzformen zur Bildung von Past, Perfect und Future

	Ersatzform	Zeiten
can	be able to	he was / has been / will be able to do
may / can	be allowed to	he was / has been / will be allowed to do
must	have (got) to	he had / has had / will have to do
will / would	be willing to	he was / has been / will be willing to do
	be prepared to	he was / has been / will be prepared to do

Merlins Zwischenprüfung

12

A. Put in the modal which fits best.

1. I think if I have a good breakfast I _____ go without food for the rest of the day. I think that until about lunchtime.
   - **a.** may
   - **c.** might
   - **b.** could
   - **d.** would

2. Different worlds – different tastes.

   "My wife has everything a man _____ want," said the tiny man from Mars. "A deep voice, broad shoulders, muscles and a moustache."
   - **a.** can
   - **c.** may
   - **b.** need
   - **d.** could

3. Mother: Ron's teacher says he _____ to have an encyclopaedia.
   Father: Nonsense. Let him walk to school like I did.
   - **a.** should
   - **c.** ought
   - **b.** need
   - **d.** must

B. Translate the German in the brackets.

1. How many psychiatrists does it take to change a light bulb?
   Only one. But the bulb (*muss wünschen*) to be changed.
2. God grant that I (*darf / könnte*) catch a fish – so big that even I when speaking of it to my friends, (*nicht brauchen / müssen*) lie.
3. Husband: I've just had a brilliant idea.
   Wife: That (*ist sicherlich*) beginner's luck.

C. What do the following modals really express?

1. She *must* be 40 years old. I counted the rings under her eyes.
   - **a.** höfliche Bitte
   - **b.** Verpflichtung
   - **c.** Schlussfolgerung

2. "Miss Smith, *would* you stop singing while you're working?"
   "Oh, I'm not working."
   - **a.** Bitte und Wunsch
   - **b.** Angebot
   - **c.** typisches Verhalten

LEVEL II : Tipps für Kenner

Mit Modals drückt man Sprechabsichten aus. Manche überschneiden sich in ihrer Bedeutung.

12

7. Erlaubnis und Verbot: can, may, must not	
Present	He can / may / is allowed to do it.
Past	He could / was allowed to do it.
Perfect	He had been allowed to do it
Verbot:	
I can't go / may not go / must not go	
I am not allowed to go	

- ✪ Da *can / could* auch Fähigkeit und Möglichkeit ausdrücken, nimmt man *to be able* beziehungsweise *to be allowed*, um Missverständnisse zu vermeiden.
- ✪ Eine typische Fehlerquelle: *you must not* heißt nicht *du musst nicht*, sondern *du darfst nicht*.
- ✪ Mit *must* geht der Zwang vom Sprecher aus. Mit *have (got) to* geht der Zwang von Dritten oder den Umständen aus.
- ✪ Nicht müssen / nicht zu tun brauchen: *he need not do it / he doesn't / didn't / won't have to do it.*

8. Vorschlagen: can, shall, must	
can't we ...?	*Can't we* dine out tonight?
couldn't he ...?	*Couldn't* Paul take us to the airport?
shall we ...?	*Shall we* go to Spain for a change?
you must ...	*You really must* see his new house.

- ✪ *Must* wird häufig durch *simply* oder *really* verstärkt.

9. Bitten: can, will		
Can you help me?	*höflicher*	Could you help me?
Will you pass me the salt?	*höflicher*	Would you pass me the salt?

Modale Hilfsverben

10. (Un-)Möglichkeit: can, could, may, might

Can	You *can't* teach an old dog new tricks.
could	The Magna Charta ensured that no free man
couldn't	*could* be hanged twice for the same offence.
may /	He *may not* be light on his feet, but he's certainly
may not	light in his head.
might /	Never argue with a fool. People *might* not know
might not	the difference.

11. Wahrscheinlichkeit: will, would, should / ought to

will	A woman who tells you her age *will* tell you everything.
would	If voting could change things it *would* be illegal.
should / ought to	Let's phone Liz up. She *ought to be* at home by now.

SPRACHFALLEN  **für Deutsche**

	Falsch	Richtig
1. Ich kann Englisch.	*I can English.*	I can *speak* English.
2. Ich kann es.	*I can it.*	I can *do* it.
3. Du musst es nicht (tun).	*You must not do it.*	You needn't *do* it.
4. Er muss es können.	*He must can it.*	He must be *able* to *do* it.
5. You must not do it.	*Du musst es nicht tun.*	Du darfst es nicht tun.

- ✪ Zu 1, 2, 3: Modals stehen selten allein. Sie werden durch ein Verb ergänzt, das im Deutschen oft wegfällt.
- ✪ Zu 4: Würden zwei Modals aufeinander treffen, nimmt man für das zweite eine Ersatzform.

Merlins Reifeprüfung

D. Put in the correct form of the modal.

12

1. Archduke Franz Ferdinand having been found alive, the first World War _____ a mistake.
   a. must be   b. needn't be   c. must have been

2. Anyone who _____ see a psychiatrist needs to have his head examined. (SAM GOLDWYN)
   a. must   b. has to   c. should

3. Old Jake went for his annual medical check-up. "Your hearing is getting worse," said the doctor. "And you _____ cut out drinking, smoking and sex."
   "What ?" cried Jake in alarm, "Just so I can hear better?"
   a. will have to   b. had to   c. should have to

E. Find the suitable modal for the German in brackets.

1. My husband is on a diet of coconuts and bananas. He hasn't lost any weight, but you (*sollen, Empfehlung*) him climbing trees.

2. Looking out of their tent Bob and Ron saw a lion. The lion was coming nearer. Bob put his jogging shoes on.
   "Why are you doing that?" Ron asked. "You won't be faster than a lion!"
   "I (*nicht müssen*) be faster then the lion," replied Bob. "I only (*nicht dürfen*) be slower than you!"

3. A wise man (*muss können*) to hire people who are wiser than himself.

F. Make your choice.

1. Bob: Ron, if you've got liver problems you *mustn't / needn't* drink any alcohol.

2. Bob: Ron, I heard you *can / can speak* Russian. Why don't you try to do business in Russia?

3. At the restaurant: "Waiter, just look at that chicken. It's nothing but skin and bones." – "*Would / will* you also like the feathers, sir?"

Merlin's saga

Our *wizened* hero **had to** take the advice of his twenty-first century friend, Bob, co-author of this potential *flop*. At the doctor's he **didn't need** to be worried. It was all very *painless*. Even so Merlin thought he **would try** to get back to his tiny apartment as quickly as **he could**. "I **could catch** the electric wagon, that *tram*, as they like to call it here."	*verhutzelt,* *Flop, Pleite* *schmerzlos* *Straßenbahn*
The whitebeard went to the kiosk to buy his tram ticket. "I **ought to** make sure that I don't have any further problems with the green uniforms", *grunted* our wizard. The tram arrived. Merlin got in and stood in the corner. "I **shouldn't have worried, should I**?" he thought to himself.	*murren, brummen*
At the next stop a blue uniform entered the tram. He came up to Merlin. "**Would you show** me your ticket, please," he *barked*. Merlin smiled. "You **must forgive** me for smiling, my dear sir," he laughed. "I was prepared for this situation." "Hey, you haven't *stamped* your ticket. You're travelling 'black'. You'll have to pay forty euros." "I didn't know", *moaned* Merlin. "I don't know how to stamp it. I'm not from here, you know." "Nonsense! A man of your age **ought to know** better. Pay your fine!" The wizard slowly lifted his *wand*.	*bellen, anschnauzen* *entwerten* *stöhnen, jammern* *Zauberstab*

12

Konditionalsätze – Conditional Sentences

CHECK your If-Clauses

Spot the mistake

a. If I would have to live my life again, I'd start making the same mistakes earlier.

b. My wife says she leaves me if I don't throw out my computer. I'll miss her.

c. Nobody is allowed to spit in a man's face unless his beard will be on fire.

 ### Tick them off

Right Wrong

a. If the Germans don't buy our English beef, we won't drink their whisky.

b. Bob, at a repair shop: Please change the oil.
Mechanic: If I would be you, I'd keep the oil and change the car.

c. If only God gave me a clear sign! Like making a large deposit in my name at a Swiss bank. (WOODY ALLEN)

d. God had never given us the bicycle, if he had wanted us to walk.

Time for a SMILE

Sam was telling Fred over a beer that he had a problem. "I'm worried, Fred," he said. "This letter came the other day and it said *if I didn't stop* making love to this bloke's wife *he was going* to kill me." "So what's the problem?" asked Fred. – "The problem? The letter wasn't signed."

Konditionalsätze

Level I : Das Einmaleins der If-Sätze

13

Typ I: Erfüllbare Bedingungen	
If-Satz: erfüllbare Bedingung	**Hauptsatz: Folgen**
a. If an experiment *works*,	something *has gone* wrong.
b. If you *want* your wife to listen,	*talk* to another woman.
Hauptsatz: Folgen	**If-Satz: erfüllbare Bedingung**
c. You *will / can* never *keep up* with somebody	if you *follow* in his footsteps.
d. Life begins at 40, but you *could miss* a lot	if you *wait* till then.

1. Im If-Satz steht eine Zeit der Gegenwart (a, b, c, d), also Present oder Present Perfect. Im If-Satz steht kein Will-Future!
2. Im Hauptsatz steht eine Verbform, die Sinn macht: zum Beispiel Present Perfect (a) oder Will-Future (c).
3. Im Hauptsatz kann auch ein Imperativ (b) oder modales Hilfsverb (c, d) wie *can, could, may* etc. stehen.
4. Der If-Satz kann auch nach dem Hauptsatz stehen (c, d).

Typ II: Nicht oder kaum erfüllbare Bedingungen	
If-Satz: Bedingung	**Hauptsatz: mögliche Folgen**
a. If the Sahara *belonged* to Russia,	within three months there *might* not *be* any sand left.
b. If the experts of the European Union bought the Sahara,	the sand in the Sahara *would double* within a year.

5. Im If-Satz steht Past Tense – nicht Konditional wie im Deutschen.
6. Im Hauptsatz kann ein modales Hilfsverb *would, could, might* + Infinitiv stehen.

ACHTUNG!

Mit Typ II spricht man nicht über die Vergangenheit, sondern über die Gegenwart (nicht erfüllbare Bedingung) oder Zukunft (theoretisch oder nur schwer erfüllbare Bedingung).

Typ III: Nicht mehr erfüllbare Bedingungen

If-Satz: Bedingung	Hauptsatz: Folgen
a. If Christopher Columbus *had not discovered* America,	he *would have saved* us a lot of trouble.
b. If Shakespeare *had had* a computer,	he *might have erased* Juliet and Romeo.

Hauptsatz: Folgen	If-Satz: Bedingung
c. Ron *could have been* a millionaire	if he *hadn't speculated* at the Stock Exchange.

13

7. Im If-Satz steht Past Perfect (a,b,c) und nicht Konditional wie im Deutschen.
    Im Hauptsatz steht Konditional II: *would have* + Partizip Perfekt
8. Im Hauptsatz steht oft *might / could* + *have* + Partizip Perfekt.

SPRACHFALLEN  für Deutsche

Deutsch	Falsch	Englisch
a. Wenn ich im Lotto gewinne	*If I'll win in the lottery ...*	If I *win* in the lottery ...
b. Wenn ich im Lotto gewinnen würde	*If I would win in the lottery ...*	If I *won* in the lottery ...
c. Wenn ich im Lotto gewonnen hätte	*If I would have won ...*	If I *had won* in the lottery ...

✪ Zu a: Kein Will-Future im If-Satz, sondern Present!
✪ Zu b: Kein Konditional I (*would do*) im If-Satz, sondern Past Tense.
✪ Zu c: Kein Konditional II (*would have done*) im If-Satz, sondern Past Perfect.

ACHTUNG! Doppeldeutige Kurzformen

Im If-Satz: *I'd, you'd, he'd* etc. = I had, you had, he had.
Im Hauptsatz: *I'd, you'd, he'd* etc. = I would, you would, he would.

Merlins Zwischenprüfung

A. Do you know a conditional sentence when you see it?

Markieren Sie Fragesatz = F, Bedingungssatz = B.

13

1. He nervously faced the boss: "My wife told me to ask you for a rise." – "Okay. I'll ask my wife *if* you can have one."

2. That's a nice hat you are wearing. I wonder *if* the style will ever come back.

3. "Why are elephants large, grey and wrinkled?" – "Well, *if* they were small, round and white they'd be aspirins."

4. When I was crossing the border into Canada, they asked *if* I had any firearms with me. I said, "Well, what do you need?"

B. Complete the following conditional sentences.

1. Sign in restaurant: If you _____ over eighty and accompanied by your parents, we will cash your cheque.

2. Security officer: Look, there is poisonous gas in this bottle. Now, what steps _____ take, if I dropped this bottle? Young scientist: Very large ones, sir!

3. We owe a lot to Edison – if it _____ for him, we'd be watching TV by candlelight. (MILTON BERLE)

4. If you are unable to decide between two things, do whichever _____ cheapest.

C. Make questions to the following answers.

There are some hints in the brackets.

1. I would take a trip around the world. (*a million pounds, win*)

2. I'd try to find another job. (*lose your job*)

3. I guess I'll take life very easy. (*get out of hospital again*)

LEVEL II : Tipps für Kenner

9. Alternativen zu *if*: Es gelten die gleichen Regeln	
provided: vorausgesetzt	Americans will eat garbage *provided* you sprinkle it liberally with ketchup.
unless: es sei denn, wenn nicht	A dress has no purpose *unless* it makes a man want to take it off. (FRANÇOISE SAGAN)
in case: falls	*In case* you need my help, give me a phone-call.

13

10. Ausnahmen: *will / would* im Bedingungssatz
a. Wenn Sie hier bitte unterschreiben *wollen / möchten / würden.*
If you *will* sign here, sir.
b. Wenn Sie so freundlich wären, mir die Tür zu öffnen.
If you *would* be so kind as to open the door for me.

✪ Im If-Satz drücken *will* und *would* eine höfliche Bitte aus.

11. *Were* oder *was* im If-Satz vom Typ II	
Schriftsprache	Umgangssprache
If I were you, I would be careful.	*If I was you*, I'd be careful.

✪ Die Konjunktivform von *be*: *I were / he, she it were* wird in der Umgangssprache zunehmend durch *I was, he, she, it was* ersetzt.

12. Kombinationen von Typ I, II und III
a. I asked her if she liked Le Corbusier and she replied, "I *would love* some – with a little lemon juice in it, if you*'ve got* any."
b. If you *had listened* to me, you *would be* rich now.
c. The dog *would not have bitten* you if you *didn't* always *kick* it.

✪ Faustregel: Im Hauptsatz steht eine Zeit, die Sinn macht.
✪ Satzzeichen: Kein Komma, wenn der Hauptsatz dem If-Satz vorangeht. Vergleiche b und c.

Merlins Reifeprüfung

D. What's your opinion?

1. If I'd got drunk last night, I would have lost my licence. *Did I lose it?*
2. I'd pay you all the money I owe you if I had any. *Have I paid the money?*
3. Unless we get a loan the company will go bankrupt. *Will the company go bankrupt?*

E. Find the full form of I'd, we'd etc.

1. I got a wonderful tribute at the airport. They fired 21 shots in the air in my honour. Of course, it would've been nicer if *they'd* waited for the plane to land.
2. Gold would never have given us the bicycle, if *he'd* wanted us to walk.
3. If *Moses'd* had a committee, the Israelites'd still be in Egypt.
4. Our modern world is so full of problems that if Moses came down from Mount Sinai again, the two tablets *he'd* be carrying would be aspirins.
5. "*What'd* you do if you found a million pounds, Mike?" asked Bridget. "Well, it all depends," said Mike, "who had lost it. Provided it was a poor person *I'd* certainly return it."

F. Which form is correct?

1. Graffiti: If I had been the Virgin Mary, I _____ "NO".
   a. had said   b. would say   c. would have said

2. A new father looking at the babies through the window of the hospital nursery: Why are they all crying? Nurse: If you _____ a few days ago without any clothes, and owed £2000 on the national debt, you would be crying, too.
   a. were born   b. had been born   c. would have been born

G. Translate the German into English.

1. It is always the best policy to tell the truth,
   vorausgesetzt, dass Sie ein ausgezeichneter Lügner sind.
2. Friendship: An emotion so sweet, steady, loyal and enduring that it
   lasts a lifetime – *es sei denn, man bittet Sie um Geld.*
3. God would never have given us the example,
   wenn er nicht gewollt hätte, dass wir an Wände schreiben.

13

H. Put in the correct forms of the Conditionals.

1. More husbands would leave home if they (*know*) how to pack their
   suitcases.
2. If you (*all stop*) talking, perhaps we could get on with the meeting.
3. If God (*be*) a Liberal, we wouldn't have the Ten Commandments –
   we'd have the Ten Suggestions.
4. Ron: What would you do in case you (*have*) rabies?
   Bob: I (*ask*) for a pencil and a sheet of paper.
   Ron: For your last will and testament?
   Bob: No, to make a list of the people I (*bite*).

Merlin's saga

13

As we *mentioned* before, living thousands of years after your time can be quite stressful. **If you knew all the problems you were going to *face*, you'd probably give up** before you began. That was not the case with Merlin. As we all know, he was a wizard and wizards don't have that sort of problem. However, there were other stresses. For example, the food. Not very healthy and a lot of fat and meat. Our white-haired hero was having nothing but problems with his *digestion*. "And I've got no magic to *cure* myself with," the *sage* moaned. **"If I had known the food tasted so bad, I would never have come** down the *ages*." One evening Bob was lying in his *deck chair* in the afternoon enjoying the sun in his back garden when he suddenly became aware of Merlin sitting on the branch of a tree. Merlin was the *size* of a *chicken*.

"Hi," said Bob. **"If you'd told me you were *dropping in*, I'd have prepared** you my super fatfree minestrone soup." The wizard placed his hand on his *stomach*. "It's a pity you didn't. I have pains every time I eat." Bob is a specialist in all these things, by the way. **"If you take my *advice*, you'll go** to my doctor. **In case you have anything serious, he'll find it.**" Merlin was interested. "What sort of *spells* does he *weave*?" Said Bob, "It's not so much a question of spells. First, you go to his *practice*. Then, **provided you have eaten nothing for two days, he will push** a *tube* down your throat, and up from the other end, too." "Holy cow," (Merlin had been watching a lot of American cowboy films), **"he'd better not do that to me, or I'll turn him** into a bottle of wine." "Sounds good to me," *chuckled* Bob to himself.

erwähnen

sich gegenübersehen

Verdauung; heilen; Weise Jahrhunderte Liegestuhl

Größe; Hühnchen; vorbei schauen Magen

Rat

Zauber; ersinnen Praxis

Schlauch

kichern

CHECK your Question Tags

 Spot the mistake

a. You are going on holiday, or?
b. I am right, amn't I?
c. Tim often comes too late, doesn't Tim?
d. There is a sauna in your hotel, isn't it?
e. Tom had an accident, hadn't he?
f. He can't have told us the truth, can't he?
g. He is never on time, isn't he?

Time for a SMILE

"Waiter, there's no chicken in my chicken soup!"
"Well, there's no horse in horseradish either, *is there?*"

Level I : Das Einmaleins der Bestätigungsfragen

14

Will man sich etwas bestätigen lassen, hängt man seiner Aussage ein *Question Tag* an. Es entspricht dem deutschen "oder", "nicht wahr".

1. "My doctor says I can't play tennis."
   "So he *has* played with you, too, *hasn't he*?"

2. "Waiter, there's a dead fly in my soup."
   "Well, for 50 pence you don't expect a dead eagle, *do you*?"

3. The oldest joke we know is when Eve asked Adam, "You love me, *don't you*?" and he replied, "Who else?"

4. Teacher: Johnny, you copied from Tom's paper, *didn't you*?
   His papers say "I don't know" and yours say "Nor do I."

✪ Hilfsverben des Aussagesatzes (*be, do, have*) und Modals (*can, must, will* etc.) werden im *tag* wiederholt.

✪ Ist das Verb bejaht, so ist das *tag* verneint. (1)

✪ Ist das Verb verneint, so ist das *tag* bejaht. (2)

✪ Vollverben im *Simple Present* und *Simple Past* werden durch *do, does, did* ersetzt. (3, 4)

✪ Das *tag* steht in der Zeit des Verbs, das es vertritt.

Intonation und Sprechabsicht

Verneintes Question Tag:

Tom lives in Egypt, *doesn't he*?
Steigend-fallende Intonation: Der Sprecher erwartet Bestätigung.

Tom lives in Egypt, *doesn't he*?
Fallend-steigende Intonation: Der Sprecher ist sich nicht sicher.

Bejahtes Question Tag:

You don't like English beer, *do you*?
Fallend-steigende Intonation: Der Sprecher ist überrascht.

Merlins Zwischenprüfung

A. Put in the appropriate Question Tag.

1. Doctor: You're troubled with sexual fantasies, _____ ?
   Patient: Oh no, doc. I rather enjoy them.

2. Woman: If I give you a fine lunch, you won't come back again, _____ ?
   Tramp: You know your cooking better than I do, ma'am.

3. The doctor was giving little Jenny a check-up:
   "Now, young lady, I'm going to take your pulse."
   "No, please don't," cried the girl. "I'll need it, _____?"

14

B. Make your choice.

1. Our chancellor is not so stupid as he seems; he couldn't be, _____ ?
   a. couldn't he   **b.** was he   **c.** could he

2. "Marriage is a lottery, _____?"
   "No, it isn't – because in a lottery you can win once in a while."
   a. is it   **b.** isn't it   **c.** isn't marriage

3. "Are you innocent or guilty?" MacTavish was asked by the judge.
   "I can't tell until I've heard the evidence, _____?" replied Mac-Tavish.
   a. can I   **b.** have I   **c.** can't I

C. Spot the mistake.

1. "Mary was a relative of yours, isn't she?"
   "Yes, she was, but she was only a very distant relative. I was my parents' first child and she was their eleventh."

2. "Your husband's a hard drinker, is he?"- "No! He finds it the easiest thing in the world."

3. "I've had my dog put to sleep."
   "It was mad, it was?"
   "Well, it wasn't too pleased."

LEVEL II : Tipps für Kenner

5. *I'm not* a fool, *am I?* **Aber:** *I'm* your best friend, *aren't I?*	*I am* wird im verneinten Question Tag zu *aren't I.*
6. There's *nobody* at home, *is there?* He *will never* marry Jane, *will he?*	Nach negativen Aussagen mit *never, no, nothing, nobody* etc. steht ein positives Question Tag.
7. *There's no* sugar in the tea, *is there?* Alan is a fool, *isn't he?*	*There* wird im Question Tag wiederholt, Namen dagegen nicht.
8. You *are* going out with Jane, *are you?*	Man verleiht so der Äußerung besonderen Nachdruck, siehe Sprachfallen.

14

SPRACHFALLEN für Deutsche

Question Tags können auch spöttische oder zweifelnde Reaktion auf Äußerungen des Gegenübers sein. Dies kann für Deutsche eine Quelle von Missverständnissen werden.

A: Tom's a genius. He's invented a Tipp-ex for computer screens.

B: Oh, he has, has he? (ironisch)

Ist der Aussagesatz bejaht, ist auch das Question Tag bejaht.

A: I don't intend to marry your daughter.

B: Oh, you don't, don't you? (Drohung)

Ist der Aussagesatz verneint, ist auch das Question Tag verneint.

✪ Die Intonationskurve ist in beiden Fällen steigend. Die deutsche Entsprechung ist "Tatsächlich? / Was Sie nicht sagen".

	Falsch	Richtig
Sie kommen doch auch, oder?	*You're coming, too, or?*	You're coming, too, *aren't you?*

✪ Eine deutsche Entsprechung für das Question Tag ist ein angehängtes "oder".

Merlins *Merlins* Reifeprüfung

D. Find a suitable Question Tag.

1. Bob was lying in his coffin and a neighbour commented on how fit and well he still looked. "He should look well, _____ ?" said his wife. "He swam one hour and jogged five miles a day."
   a. doesn't he   b. should he   c. shouldn't he

14

2. Mike went to the doctor and told him he was suffering from halluci-nations, "Nonsense, man," said the doctor, "you're imagining things, _____ ?"
   a. are you   b. don't you   c. aren't you

3. A hedgehog finding himself on top of a scrubbing brush: Well, I am a fool _____ ?
   a. aren't I   b. amn't I   c. Am I not

E. Choose the Question Tag.

1. "I intend to marry your daughter next week."
   Angry father: _____ ?
   a. Oh, you do, don't you?   b. Oh, you do, do you?

2. Passenger on the train: I can't pay for my ticket today.
   Ticket inspector: Oh, you can't, _____ ?
   a. can't you   b. can you

3. Policeman: Show me your driving licence.
   Driver: I haven't got it with me.
   Policeman: Oh, you haven't, _____ ?
   a. haven't you   b. have you

F. There are some Question Tags that are more difficult. Use the key to get to know them.

1. Son: Mum, I needn't go to school today, _____ ? All the teachers hate me and so do the children.
   Mum: But you must go, son. After all, you are the headmaster.

2. "You'd better pay attention, _____ ? You're driving on the pavement." "Oh, I thought you were driving."

3. You'd rather go, _____ ?

4. Please be quiet, _____ ?

5. He never used to be so fat, _____ ?

Merlin's saga

So Merlin decided to do something about his *health.*   *Gesundheit*
What did he do? Of course, he looked into going to a
health farm, **didn't he**? Where he gets all his money

14   from, I don't know. It was *somewhere* in the south of the   *irgendwo*
River *Danube*. Here's Merlin's story: *Donau*

    Merlin arriving at the hotel:
Receptionist: I can't help you in some way, sir, **can I**?
Merlin: Well, you're expecting me for the week, **aren't
    you**?
Receptionist: What is the name, sir?   *Zauberer*
Merlin: Merlin, the *magician.*
Receptionist: Yes, Mr Merlin Magician. That's the
    name, **isn't it**?
Merlin: Well, more or less.
Receptionist: Yes, you're in room 215. Here's the key.
    You can take the lift.

    In the sports and wellness room:
Masseur (*slapping* Merlin's neck aggressively):   *klatschen*
    My God, you've been *neglecting* yourself, **haven't**   *vernachlässigen*
    you? You're all *skin and bones*. No muscles left.   *Haut und Kno-*
    What have you been doing with yourself in the last   *chen*
    few years?
Merlin (*grunting* in pain): Last few years? You mean the   *stöhnen*
    last few hundred years, **don't you**?
Masseur: *You ought to* see a doctor. Last few hundred   *Sie sollten*
    years? You'd be dead, **wouldn't you**?
Merlin: Right, young man. I think you need some
    information and some respect for your *elders*,   *ältere Leute*
    don't you? Look into this mirror, and you will
    understand.

Relativsätze – Relative Clauses

CHECK your Relatives

 Spot the mistake

a. A coward is a man in who the instinct of self-preservation acts normally.
b. Culture is anything what we do and what the monkeys don't.
c. A theologian is a blind man in a dark room who is searching for a black cat who is not there – and he finds it.

 Tick them off   **Right   Wrong**

a. A pedestrian is a man who has a car and his son is home from college.
b. A friend is someone, who dislikes the same people as you.
c. Planning is the art of putting off until tomorrow which you have no intention of doing today.
d. Life is that what happens while you are making other plans. (JOHN LENNON)
e. The honeymoon is the period during which the bride trusts the bridegroom's word of honour.

Time for a SMILE

> A neurotic is a person *who* builds a castle in the air.
> A psychotic is the person *who* lives in it.
> A psychiatrist is the one *who* collects the rent.
> (JEROME LAWRENCE)

LEVEL I

Level I : Das Einmaleins der Relativpronomen

15

Type I: Der notwendige Relativsatz

Mit einem Relativpronomen (zum Beispiel *who*) verbindet man zwei Hauptsätze (a und b) zu einem Relativsatz (c).

- **a.** A striptease dancer is a girl.
- **b.** She has everything and shows it.
- **c.** A striptease dancer is a *girl who* has everything and shows it.

Das Relativpronomen (*who)* bezieht sich auf sein Bezugswort (*girl*) und definiert es näher. Type I heißt "notwendig" (*defining*), weil ohne ihn die Information nicht komplett ist. Vor dem Relativpronomen steht kein Komma.

Die Relativpronomen in Typ I

Bezugswort ist	A. Umgangssprache		B. Formelle Sprache	
	Person	Sache	Person	Sache
1. Subjekt	who / that	which/that	who	which
2. Objekt	(who / that)[1]	(that)[1]	whom	which
3. Objekt mit Präposition	who / that + preposition	that	preposition + whom	which
4. Zugehörigkeit	whose (+ preposition)		(preposition +) whose	

Zu 1: An alcoholic is *someone who* drinks more than his doctor. (A und B)
Zu 2: Experience is the *name (that / which)* we give to our mistakes. (A und B)
Zu 3: Dentists and lawyers are the *people to whom* we always show our best side. (B)
Zu 4: Concerts and theatre: *People whose* seats are in the middle of the row always arrive last. (A und B)

---

1 Das Relativpronomen fällt in der Umgangssprache meist weg, siehe Seite 110

Merlins *Merlins* Zwischenprüfung

A. Identify which type they are.

1. *Which* way do you think is the quickest to the town centre?
   - **a.** question word
   - **b.** relative pronoun

2. According to the latest statistics there are almost five million Germans *who* aren't working. And there are even more if you count those with jobs.
   - **a.** question word
   - **b.** relative pronoun

3. Automatic: That *which* you can't repair yourself.
   - **a.** question word
   - **b.** relative pronoun

15

B. Put in the correct Pronoun.

1. A baby is an angel _____ wings decrease as his legs increase.

2. A husband is someone _____ will share with you all the problems you wouldn't have had in the first place, if you had not married him.

3. Any programme _____ depends on human reliability is unreliable.

C. Use a suitable Relative to join the sentences.

1. A pessimist is a man. He thinks all women are bad. An optimist hopes so.

2. An acquaintance is a person. We know him well enough to borrow money from him, but not well enough to lend him money.

3. A tree is an object. It will stand in one place for years and then suddenly jump in front of a lady driver.

Relativsätze

LEVEL II

LEVEL II : Tipps für Kenner

15

Type II: Der nicht notwendige Relativsatz

Er heißt "nicht notwendig" (*non-defining*), weil man ihn weglassen kann, ohne dass der Satz sinnlos wird. Er gehört der Schriftsprache an. Vor dem Pronomen steht Komma oder Gedankenstrich.

Die Relativpronomen in Typ II

Bezugswort ist	A. Person	B. Sache
1. Subjekt	,who	,which
2. Objekt	,whom	,which
3. Objekt mit Präposition	preposition +	
	,whom	,which
4. Zugehörigkeit	,whose	,whose
5. ein Satz / Gedanke	,which	

Zu 1: I flew over on Concorde, *which is a plane* that is so fast that you have an extra couple of hours to look for your luggage. (B 1)

Zu 2: He is an unpleasant fellow, *whom* you never see, but who is nevertheless spreading gossip. (A 2)

Zu 3: To get something done a committee should consist of no more than three men, *two of whom* are absent. (A 3)

Zu 4: A baby, *whose* father could not be identified, was found at the railway station. (A 4)

Zu 5: Jesus loves you, *which shows* that he has a good sense of humour. (A und B 5)

6. Relativsätze ohne Pronomen – Contact Clauses

If you want to know what God thinks of money, look at the people **a.** *who* he gives it *to.* / **b.** he *gives* it *to.*

Who, whom, which und *that* können wegfallen (**b**), wenn sie Objekt sind. Präpositionen stehen hinter dem Verb.

SPRACHFALLEN  für Deutsche

Deutsch	Falsch	Englisch
1. Ich habe ihn nie ge-troffen, *was* schade ist.	*I've never met him, what is a pity.*	I've never met him, *which* is a pity.
2. Sag mir alles, *was* du weißt.	*Tell me all what you know.*	Tell me all (*that*) you know.
3. Sag mir, *was* du weißt.	*Tell me which you know.*	Tell me *what* you know.
4. Das ist etwas, *was* wir brauchen.	*That's something what we need.*	That's something (*that*) we need.
5. Ihr gefiel nicht, *was* ich sagte.	*She didn't like which I said.*	She didn't like *what* I said.

✪ Zu 1: Relativpronomen *was* bezieht sich auf einen ganzen Satz bezie-hungsweise Gedanken, es entspricht *which* mit Komma.

✪ Zu 2: Anders als im Deutschen kann *what* nicht in Relativsätzen vom Typ I oder II stehen. Vergleiche 3 und 5.

✪ Zu 3 und 5: *What* steht in "Relativsätzen" ohne Bezugswort bezie-hungsweise ohne Gedanken, auf den es sich beziehen könnte.

✪ Zu 4: Das Relativpronomen *what*:

> Basic research is *what* I'm doing when I don't know what I'm doing. (Wernher von Braun)

> Since a politician never believes *what* he says, he is always astonished when others do. (CHARLES DE GAULLE)

What kann sich *nicht* auf ein Bezugswort (*all, something, everything* etc.), einen ganzen Satz oder Gedanken beziehen. Ist ein Bezug vor-handen, nehmen wir eines der anderen Relativpronomen.

Merlins Reifeprüfung

15

D. Use Relative Pronouns instead of dashes (*Gedankenstriche*).

1. Englishmen hate two things – they are racial discrimination and Irishmen.
2. Do you remember Jack – he died with his boots on? One was on the accelerator.
3. Friendship is like money – easier made than kept.

E. Make your choice.

1. This April 1st is the day upon which we are reminded _____ we are on the other 364. (MARK TWAIN)

   a. of that   b. of what

2. Doctors pour drugs _____ they know little,
   to cure disease _____ they know less,
   into human beings _____ they know nothing.

   a. of whom   b. of which
   c. which   d. of which
   e. of whom   f. of whose

F. Put in the commas where necessary.

1. There are more men than women in mental hospitals which just goes to show who's driving whom crazy.
2. Concorde travels at twice the speed of sound which is fun except that you can't hear the movie until two hours after you land.
3. Farmer Jack's special chicken which lays rectangular eggs cost him nearly £ 500. "That's an expensive chicken," he said to the shop assistant. "I hope it can speak as well." – "Of course, but it says only one word." – "And what's that?" – "Ouch!"

G. Choose the Relative Pronoun.

1. I've never visited China, *what / which* is a thing I've always wanted to do.
2. Her boss really didn't like *that what / what* she said to him.
3. If you tell me *what / all what* you know, I may let you go free.

Merlin's saga

Merlin was beginning to feel that the things he was doing here in the twenty-first century were *worthwhile* after all. He had indeed managed to help some people **who** had been *experiencing* real problems. The old gentleman was walking on a path along the side of the river **that** had become a favourite area of his. He became aware of a *sobbing* sound **which** was coming from behind a tree. He *wondered* **whose** life could be so miserable as to *cause* such a reaction. He *hobbled* round the tree, the *trunk* **of which** was two metres thick. And there he saw her, a girl of about nineteen years. She had brown eyes, both **of which** were full of tears. The wizard touched her shoulder with his *wand*, **from which** a *spark* jumped. "Now, my dear, first calm yourself," **which** she did immediately as soon as the magic entered her *soul*. "Now, tell me what troubles you?" "I've got my exams tomorrow and I'm having a blackout, **which** means I'll *fail* the exams. Then I can't go to university, I won't become a doctor." "There are more important things than exams," *whispered* the whitebeard. "Think of your health, and the health and *joy* of your friends and family, **who** are around you even during bad times. Life is what you make of it. Don't fight against those parts of life **that** seem unfriendly. Take it all as a life *experience*." Merlin walked over to the river, took out a half coconut *shell* **which** was hanging under his cloak and *scooped* out a mixture of *mud* and water. "Here drink this." "Hggh," thought the girl. But she drank it anyway. The *potion*, the last drop **of which** somehow even tasted good, was called Merlin's cava. Her *fear* disappeared with the muddy liquid.

der Mühe wert

durchmachen

15

schluchzen

sich fragen; verursachen; humpeln; Stamm

Zauberstab; Funke

Seele

durchfallen

flüstern

Freude

Erfahrung
Schale
schöpfen
Schlamm
Trank
Angst

Der Infinitiv mit und ohne "to" – The Infinitive with and without "to"

CHECK CHECK your Infinitives

 Spot the mistake

a. An adult is somebody who has stopped to grow vertically but not horizontally.
b. The formula for failure – try pleasing everyone.
c. He may drink to forget, but he never forgets drinking.
d. Small boy watching his Mum to do the washing: "Mum, where did you work before you got this job here with us?"

 Tick them off　　　　　　　　　**Right　Wrong**

a. "Why are you jumping up and down like that?" – "Because I've just taken some medicine and I forgot to shake the bottle."
b. Yesterday I went to the doctor about my bad memory. He made me to pay in advance.
c. Have you heard about the Scotsman who took his wife's false teeth to work with him every day to stop her eating between meals?
d. Most of those who would like moving mountains don't like practising on the little hills.

Time for a SMILE

At an evening party the hostess talked a protesting guest into singing. After the song, she went up to him and said with a smile, "Oh dear, Mr Jenkins, you *need never tell* me again that you *can't sing*. I know it now."

LEVEL I
Level I : Das Einmaleins des Infinitivs

A. Der Infinitiv ohne *to*

1. Der Infinitiv ohne *to* steht nach

have / make someone do something	veranlassen, dazu bringen
let someone do something	erlauben, zulassen

16

A theatre critic wrote about a new play: I suggest that the author should make a few changes. In the last act where he *has* the wife *stab* her husband, he should *make* her *shoot* him with a revolver. It will not only wake the audience, but also *let* them *know* that the show is over.

2. Der Infinitiv ohne *to* steht nach

I / You had better	es wäre besser, wenn ich / du
I / You would rather	ich würde / du würdest lieber

Driving instructor: You'*d better pay* attention. You're driving on the pavement.
Learner: Oh, I thought you were driving.

The trouble with most of us is that we *would rather be* ruined with praise than saved by criticism.

3. Der Infinitiv ohne *to* steht nach

modalen Hilfsverben (*modals: can, may, must, shall, will*)

Achtung: Nach den Ersatzformen (*be able to, be allowed to, have to*) steht der Infinitiv jedoch mit *to*.

Ausnahme: Nach *ought* steht der Infinitiv mit *to*.

Any fool *can paint* a picture, but it takes a wise man to *be able to sell it*. (SAMUEL BUTLER)
There's one thing you *ought not to do* in a submarine: Sleep with the windows open.

Der Infinitiv mit und ohne "to"

B. Der Infinitiv mit *to*

1. Der Infinitiv mit *to* steht nach

- ☻ bestimmten Adjektiven und Substantiven
- ☻ Superlativen *the first / the last / the best* + Substantiv und ähnlichen Ausdrücken wie *the only* + Substantiv
- ☻ Fragewörtern *where to go, what to do, which film to see* etc., oft zur Bitte um Instruktionen
- ☻ als Subjekt, häufig am Satzanfang

It's *easy to be* a humorist when you have the whole government working for you. (WILL ROGERS)

What's the *best way to get* in touch with your long-lost relatives? – Win the lottery.

The *first man to tear* a telephone book in half probably had teenage kids.

He taught his wife *how to play* poker and won back half of his salary.

To err is human – *to blame* it on someone else is even more human.

2. Der Infinitiv mit *to* steht nach

- ☻ Verben des Wünschens und Wollens wie *want, like, wish, prefer, intend, need*
- ☻ Verben des Zulassens und Veranlassens wie *allow, cause, decide, expect, order, permit, tell someone to do something*
- ☻ Ausdrücken mit *for*: *a book for you to read, wait for the police to arrive, easy for Paul to understand*

If you *want your wife to listen*, then talk to another woman.

A doctor is a man who can *tell a woman to take off* her clothes and send her husband a bill for it.

Otto is the most common name in Ostfriesland because there are only *two letters for the parents to remember*.

Merlins Zwischenprüfung

A. Make your choice.

1. You can *lead / to lead* a horse to water, but you can't *make / to make* it drink.

2. Bob was the first man in Barbados *to make / make* a million dollars.

16

3. Please let me *drive / to drive* the car. Nobody's looking.

B. Put "to" into the sentences where necessary.

1. Nothing is illegal if a hundred businessmen decide _____ do it.

2. If you want _____ forget all your troubles, wear a pair of tight shoes.

3. I'd rather _____ have my peace and quiet than all this stress.

C. Translate the German in the brackets.

1. Some people would (*es vorziehen zu sein*) wrong than to keep quiet.

2. (*Es wäre besser, wenn du*) learn to swim if you're going on a sailing holiday.

3. An optimist is a man who goes into a restaurant, orders oysters, and (*erwartet*) pay the bill with the pearls he'll find inside them.

Der Infinitiv mit und ohne "to"

LEVEL II : Tipps für Fortgeschrittene

A. Infinitiv ohne *to* oder *-ing*-Form

1. Sinnliche Wahrnehmung

Nach Verben wie *see, feel, hear, watch, notice* steht
- ✪ Infinitiv ohne *to* für abgeschlossene oder aufeinander folgende Handlungen oder
- ✪ Partizip Präsens (*-ing-form*), wenn man den Ablauf der Handlung betonen will. Der Bedeutungsunterschied ist jedoch gering.

To *see* a man *do* a good deed is to forget all his faults.
It's no fun going to the airline desk to complain about lost luggage only to *see* the clerk *wearing* your clothes.

B. Infinitiv mit *to* oder *-ing*-Form

1. Vorliebe und Abneigung

Nach Ausdrücken wie *like, love, prefer, be keen, hate, want* steht
- ✪ Infinitiv mit *to* – meist für einen Einzelfall oder
- ✪ Gerund – meist für Regelfälle beziehungsweise Gewohnheiten.

One actress to another: "I've heard so much about your love-making. Now I *want to hear* your side of the story."
All things I *like doing* are either immoral, illegal or fattening.
(OSCAR WILDE)

---

2. Anfangen, Fortdauern, Aufhören

- ✪ Nach Verben wie *begin, start / continue / cease* steht Infinitiv mit *to* oder Gerund.

Middle age is when your age *starts to show* around the middle.
Start filling my bag up with money or you'll be sorry!

LEVEL III : Tipps für Kenner

Bedeutungsunterschiede zwischen Infinitiv und Gerund

1. stop to do something — anhalten, um etwas zu tun
   stop doing something — aufhören, etwas zu tun

2. try to do something — versuchen, etwas zu tun
   try doing something — etwas ausprobieren

3. mean to do something — beabsichtigen, etwas zu tun
   mean doing something — etwas bedeuten

4. forget to do something — vergessen, etwas zu tun
   forget doing something — vergessen, dass man etwas getan hat

5. remember to do something — daran denken, etwas zu tun
   remember doing something — sich erinnern, etwas getan zu haben

A passer-by saw a boy trying to reach a door-bell. He *stopped to ring* the bell for the boy. "Thank you, sir," said the boy, "but now we'd both better run for it."

Holiday is the day when a man *stops doing* what his boss wants and *starts doing* what his wife wants.

"Doc! Whenever I *try to drink* tea my eye hurts. What shall I do?" Doctor: Hmmm! *Try taking* the spoon out of the glass!

Death *means stopping* sinning suddenly.

If God *meant us to be* homosexuals he would have created Adam and Eric.

"Why is James sticking his tongue out?"
"I guess the doctor *forgot to tell* him to put it back in."

Daddy, do you *remember saying* you'd give me £10 for passing my exams? Well, you don't have to pay me now.

SPRACHFALLEN für Deutsche

Auf die Stellung kommt es an:

He wanted to marry *her*.	Er wollte *sie* heiraten.
He wanted *her* to marry.	Er wollte, *dass sie* heiratet.
He wanted *her* to marry *him*.	Er wollte, *dass sie ihn* heiratet.

Der Infinitiv mit und ohne "to"

16

D. -ing-form or Infinitive?

1. The formula for failure – try _____ everybody.
   a. to please   b. pleasing

2. Try not _____ a man of success but rather try _____ a man of value. (ALBERT EINSTEIN)
   a. to become   b. becoming

3. If you think nothing is impossible, try _____ your name off a mailing list.
   a. to get   b. getting

E. Make your choice.

1. I much prefer *to travel / travelling* in non-British ships. There's none of the nonsense about women and children first. (S. MAUGHAM)

2. Customer: I'm thinking of buying a Rolls Royce. Can you tell me the annual cost of running one?
   Salesman: Anyone who needs *to ask / asking* a question like that, sir, can't afford one.

3. Don't forget *to imitate / imitating* the behaviour of winners when you lose. (GEORGE MERIDITH)

F. Spot the mistake.

1. If you want knowing the value of money, go and try to borrow some.

2. Ron: I hate paying my income tax.
   Bob: Be a good citizen. Why don't you pay with a smile?
   Ron: I would like to, but they insist on money.

3. She: I've just read an interesting article. It said that most accidents that happen, happen in the kitchen.
   He: I know and you expect me eating them.

Merlin's saga

Like everybody else around this place Merlin is getting older (perhaps we don't notice him *aging* since it happens more slowly to him as a wizard), but *in any case* people who have birthdays **like to** get invited out. And so it was with Merlin.

altern
auf jeden Fall

Although he **hadn't wanted to** mention it to Ron and Bob they had found it out in an ancient library. He *denied* being more than fifteen hundred years old, but that didn't help. Bob and Ron **wished to** invite him to a good meal in a typical, local restaurant.

obwohl;
abstreiten

Bob, Ron and Merlin:

B: Well, what can we **offer** you **to drink** on this special *occasion*, old wizard?

Gelegenheit

M: My goodness me, it seems like *millennia* ago that I had a real *mead* or an ale. I **remember spending** many a good evening with my favourite witch. I ...

Jahrtausende
Honigwein/Bier

R: (*interrupting*) You'll enjoy drinking some modern *brews* as well. What **you'd better try** is a *mulled wine* since there's snow still on the ground.

Gebräu;
Glühwein

M: Ah yes, hot wine with *spice* like in the old, old days. Imagine sitting at the *jousts*! And a hot red wine and hot red-haired witch next to you.

Gewürze
Turnier

B: Here's the mulled wine with turbo.

M: More modern mechanics? What has wine to do with *engines?* Excuse me saying so, but you moderns have a complex about machinery. In my day we **tried to live** naturally.

Motor, Maschine

R: Calm down, Merlin. **Let** us **show** you what our turbo is. Taste this drink.

M: Hmm, that's more like a good old grog. The magic's in the glass. It gives me power.

B: That's it. You've got a turbo charge. You're on turbo power.

M: **Let me have** another glass. It's just right for a modern wizard. Gazumppp!

Das Gerund, die andere "ing"-Form – The Gerund, the other "ing" form

C H E C K CHECK your Gerunds

 Spot the mistake

a. If at first you don't succeed, try, try again. Then give up. It's no use to be a damned fool about it. (W. C. FIELDS)

b. When in Paris, I always eat at the Eiffel Tower restaurant because it's the only place where I can avoid to see the damned thing. (WILLIAM MORRIS)

c. Most of those who would like moving mountains don't like practising on the little hills.

 Tick them off   **Right Wrong**

a. Imagine the whole world being created in six days! Fortunately we now have the trade unions.

b. Can you imagine to live in a city entirely under glass? We'd never have to worry about cold or rain or snow again. Just little kids with rocks!

c. I used to suffer from a split personality, Doc, but now we're both okay!

d. I'll never get used to living in a big city.

e. Nothing worth learning is learned quickly, except parachuting.

Time for a SMILE

The little devils *propose having* a football match against the little angels. "OK," say the angels, "but you know very well that we have the best players."
"Possibly," answer the devils, "but we've got the referees."

The Gerund, the other "ing" form

LEVEL I : Das Einmaleins des Gerunds

1. Formen

✪ An die Grundform (Infinitiv) wird *-ing* angehängt.
✪ Stummes *e* am Ende fällt weg.
✪ Der Endkonsonant wird nach kurzem betontem Vokal verdoppelt.

17

sleep – sleeping   write – writing   swim – swimming

Being married to a woman means
seeing her in the morning instead of in the evening.

2. Funktionen

Das Gerund ist wie das Present Participle eine *-ing*-Form. Es unterscheidet sich vom Partizip durch seine Funktionen im Satz.

Das Gerund als

a. Subjekt	*Planning* means replacing chance by error.
b. Objekt	Credit cards have made *buying* easier but *paying* harder.
c. Prädikat	The hardest thing about boxing *is picking* up your teeth with a boxing glove on.
d. mit eige-nem Subjekt	I don't like *my son / him watching* television all the time.

3. Wann nehmen wir Gerund?

a. Das Gerund steht nach bestimmten Verben:

avoid	vermeiden	imagine	sich vorstellen
enjoy	genießen	mind	etwas haben gegen,
excuse	entschuldigen	miss	verpassen, versäumen
dislike	nicht mögen	risk	riskieren, wagen
finish	beenden	suggest	vorschlagen

Das Gerund, die andere "ing"-Form

17

b. Das Gerund steht nach Präpositionen:

Clarity is the ability to give directions *without taking* your hands out of your pockets.

A Los Angeles bank robber made a serious mistake *after obtaining* cash from the bank clerk. *Instead of grabbing* the money and *running*, he told the clerk to deposit it in his own account.

c. Das Gerund steht nach Verben, Adjektiven und Substantiven, die eine Präposition nach sich haben:

Verb + Präposition

succeed *in marketing* a product	ein Produkt mit Erfolg vermarkten
look forward *to meeting* him	sich freuen, ihn kennen zu lernen
insist *on being* paid	darauf bestehen, bezahlt zu werden

A diplomat is a man who can tell you to go to hell in such a way that you actually look forward *to going on* the trip.

Adjektiv + Präposition

I'm *interested in improving* my English.	Ich interessiere mich dafür, mein Englisch zu verbessern.
He's *good at skiing*.	Er kann gut Ski fahren.
We're *proud of being* the best.	Ich bin stolz, der Beste zu sein.

One door-to-door salesman does very well by using the opening line: "Are you *interested in possessing* something which your neighbour said you couldn't possibly afford?"

Substantiv + Präposition

have *difficulty in doing* something	Schwierigkeiten mit etwas haben
the *idea of doing* something	der Gedanke, etwas zu tun
the *art of managing* people	die Kunst der Menschenführung

Psychiatrist: Do you *have difficulty in making* up your mind?
Patient: Well, yes and no.

The Gerund, the other "ing" form

Merlins **Zwischenprüfung**

A. Infinitive or Gerund.

1. Policeman: You were doing 5 m.p.h.

   Motorist: Would you mind *putting / to put* 90 m.p.h. on the form?
   I'd like to show it to the man I'm selling it to.

2. Boss: What do you mean by arguing with that customer?
   Don't you know the rule? The customer is always right.

   Assistant: I know. But he insisted on *being / to be* wrong.

3. My way *to joke / of joking* is to tell the truth.

B. Translate the words in the brackets.

1. "I (*möchte*) buy my girlfriend a ring, but I don't know what she'd
   like." – "Does she like you?" – "Of course!" – "Then she would like
   anything."

2. Time is nature's way (*zu verhindern*), (*dass alles gleichzeitig geschieht*).

3. The art of medicine (*besteht darin, den Patienten zu amüsieren*) while
   nature cures the disease. (VOLTAIRE)

C. Put in the correct form.

1. _____ is something you should not do, if you want to be a
   competitive athlete.
   a. To smoke   **b.** Smoking   **b.** Having smoked

2. He's very good _____. That's why he became a salesman.
   a. at talking   **b.** in talking   **b.** to talk

3. That was a pleasant phone-call. I look forward _____ you later.
   a. to see   **b.** see   **b.** to seeing

Das Gerund, die andere "ing"–Form

17

4. Idiomatische Ausdrücke, die Gerund nach sich haben

It's no use trying.	Es hat keinen Zweck, es zu versuchen.
It's no good complaining.	Es nützt nichts, sich zu beschweren.
It's (not) worth doing.	Es lohnt sich (nicht), es zu tun.
There is no knowing what may happen.	Man kann nie wissen, was passiert.
What / how about going for a walk?	Wie wäre es mit einem Spaziergang?

5. Infinitiv oder Gerund: kein Bedeutungsunterschied[1]

✪ Infinitiv mit *to* oder Gerund nach Verben des Anfangens (*begin, start*), des Fortdauerns (*continue*), des Aufhörens (*finish, cease*)

Middle age is when you *start to plan* the evening with TV magazine.

If I had my life to live over again, I'd *start making* the same mistakes earlier.

6. Infinitiv oder Gerund: geringer Bedeutungsunterschied

✪ Nach den Ausdrücken der Vorliebe und Abneigung (*like, love, prefer, be keen, be interested, hate*) steht
✪ Infinitiv mit *to* – meist für einen Einzelfall oder
✪ Gerund – meist für Regelfälle beziehungsweise Gewohnheiten
✪ Merke: *I'd like* nur mit *to* + Infinitiv

Reporter to Minister of Defence: "We've heard so much about your love-making, now I'd *like to hear* your side of the story."

All things I *like doing* are either immoral, illegal or fattening.
(OSCAR WILDE)

---

1 Siehe auch Kapitel: Der Infinitiv mit und ohne "to", Seite 118.

The Gerund, the other "ing" form

7. Infinitiv mit *to* und Gerund mit unterschiedlicher Bedeutung

try to do something	versuchen, etwas zu tun
try doing something	etwas ausprobieren / versuchen mit …
go on to do something	sich anschicken, etwas zu tun
go on doing something	etwas weiterhin tun, fortfahren mit

If you want to know the value of money, go and *try to borrow* some.
(BENJAMIN FRANKLIN)

Not only is there no God, but *try getting* a plumber at weekends.
(WOODY ALLEN)

8. Pronomen und Substantive vor Gerund

Formelle Sprache:	I don't mind	Peter's *coming* to the party
		his
Informelle Sprache:	I don't mind	Peter *coming* to the party
		him

SPRACHFALLEN  für Deutsche

a. Die Präposition *to* ist nicht immer Signal für Infinitiv.

I used to live in a big city.	Ich wohnte früher …

Aber:

I'm used to living in a big city.	Ich bin gewohnt zu …
I'll never get used to living in a big city.	Ich werde mich nie an … gewöhnen

Merke auch: I'm looking *forward to meeting* Tamara.

b. Vorsicht vor Missverständnissen.

Tom: Do you like *cleaning* ladies?
Tim: I don't know, I've never *cleaned* one.

Merlins Reifeprüfung

D. Match the meanings against the forms.

1. I stopped helping Mary. She was too difficult.
   a. Ich habe aufgehört, ihr zu helfen.
   b. Ich hielt an, um ihr zu helfen.

2. The policeman went on examining the criminal.
   a. Der Polizist schickte sich an, ihn zu überprüfen.
   b. Der Polizist fuhr mit der Überprüfung fort.

3. I propose to leave Germany and live on an island.
   a. Ich habe die Absicht, Deutschland zu verlassen.
   b. Ich schlage vor, Deutschland zu verlassen.

E. "Used to" or "am used to -ing"?

1. I _____ a werewolf, but I'm alright nooooooow!
   a. used to be   b. am used to being

2. Anita was so mean she _____ the knives so the family would use less butter.
   a. was used to heating   b. used to heat

3. I _____ arrogant. Now I'm perfectly okay.
   a. used to be   b. am used to being

F. Spot the mistake.

Bob: Ron, I'm going to run in the Heidelberg Marathon.

Ron: Are you crazy? You'll risk to get a heart attack.

Bob: Rubbish. You know I enjoy to run in the open air. There's nothing better.

Ron: But you intended doing that competition next year. What changed your mind?

Bob: Ron, it's very easy. I don't want to miss to eat my fill at the "Pasta Party" the day before.

Merlin's saga

As we have already heard, Merlin was *overworked* and *exhausted*. "**Working** all the time and especially arguing with the 'moderns' destroys one's health," thought the wizard to himself. "I'm very *keen on* **travelling** back two thousand years for a short holiday. I like **visiting** new places and times, but there's nothing like home." And so it *came to pass* that Merlin was sitting in a wonderfully warm *cave* with his favourite *witch* discussing the future.	*überarbeitet* *erschöpft*
	scharf auf
	geschehen *Höhle; Hexe*
W: Well, old Merlin, you're certainly risking **losing** a lot of *weight* if the food is as bad as you say in the twenty-first century.	*Gewicht*
M: You've really put your finger on a problem there. Look at this young wild *pig* turning gently over the fire. What a taste! I really *appreciate* **eating** the flesh, **smelling** the aroma. In the twenty-first century they eat pills and tablets. They even try not **eating** at all to become thin. They think it's beautiful. I hate **digging** my meat out of metal boxes. They call them "tins".	*Schwein* *schätzen*
	Ausgraben *Blechdose*
W: How depressing! I hope the ales are drinkable at least.	
M: Oh, they have hundreds of beers and hundreds of *rules* and *laws* about **drinking** beer. But in the end those liquids are watery and tasteless. Can you believe that in Germania, where I live, you get a yellow beer and they take seven minutes to *pour* it out.	*Regel; Gesetz*
	hier: zapfen

17

CHECK your Participles

18

Spot the mistake

a. Tim was swiming in the pool.
b. I watched the blond girl arresting by the detective.
c. Behind every successful man is a woman wanted a fur coat.
d. I heard the phone ringing only once.

Tick them off

Right Wrong

a. I watched the sun setting behind the mountain.
b. I watched the boats sail out of the harbour.
c. They remained seated and eated at the table.
d. Gentlemen, please remain seated.
e. The country lay covering in snow.
f. The dog lay dying on the road.

Time for a SMILE

A couple *walking* in the park noticed a young man and woman *sitting* on a bench, *kissing* passionately.
"Why don't you do that?" said the wife.
"But darling," replied her husband, "I don't even know that woman!"

LEVEL I : Das Einmaleins der Partizipien

1. Formen

Present Participle = aktiver Sinn	**asking**
Past Participle = passiver Sinn	**asked**

Dignity of labour is an idea *invented* (b) by politicians *trying* (a) to cut back on welfare[1].

a. Das Present Participle hat aktive Bedeutung:
politicians *trying* = politicians *who were / are trying.*

b. Das Past Participle hat passive Bedeutung:
an idea *invented* = an idea *which was invented.*

c. Mit Partizipien verkürzt man notwendige Relativsätze. Relativpronomen und Formen von *to be* werden weglassen.

d. Partizipien verkürzen auch adverbiale Nebensätze, die sagen, was *wann, wie, warum, womit* geschieht oder geschehen ist.

2. Partizipialkonstruktionen: Verkürzte Nebensätze

a. der Zeit: *when, as soon as, while*	Barking dogs don't bite – while *barking.* (... *while they are barking*)
b. der Art und Weise: *as if, thus*	Industry prefers teamwork [*thus*] *allowing* managers to put the blame on their colleagues.
c. des Zugeständnisses: *though, although* (*Although man is seated* ...)	[*Although*] *Seated* on the highest throne in the world, man is still sitting on his behind.
d. der Bedingung: *if, provided* *enough time and money*)	Any technical problem can be overcome *given* enough time and money. (... *if you are given*
e. des Grundes: *because, as, since*	Dogs in Saudi Arabia are the fastest – the trees *being* so far apart. (*because the trees are ...*)

✪ Die Konjunktionen (a – d) *können* bei Verkürzung wegfallen. Zur Vermeidung von Missverständnissen behält man sie oft bei.

✪ Es *müssen* wegfallen: die Konjunktionen des Grundes (e).

1 dignity of labour: Würde der Arbeit; cut back on welfare: Sozialleistungen kürzen

Merlins Zwischenprüfung

A. Use a Relative Clause instead of the Participle.

Careful with the Tenses.

18

1. The detective wanted to have a word with Merlin *standing* next to the bar.
2. He thought Merlin could help him to find the pictures *stolen* from the museum.
3. Merlin led him to a street map *hanging* on the wall, murmured a few words and with his wand he made a cross on it.

B. Identify the Participles.

1. An oyster is a fish *built / building* like a nut.
2. Tony: Why did you give up your boyfriend?
   Tina: I saw him *sunbathing / sunbathed* and he looked so different without his wallet.
3. A consultant is a man (or woman) *calling / called* in to share the blame.

C. Replace the Participles. Use a suitable Conjunction.

1. Weather permitting, we'll go for a walk.
2. He took no notice of us, being interested in what was happening at the other side of the street.
3. Walking through the park, we had a lively discussion.

D. Translate the German in the brackets.

Words to help you:

to rush in, to frustrate, to move

1. I was teaching my girlfriend the tango when her father (*kam herein-gestürzt*). How was I to know he was stone deaf?
2. The Health Minister, visiting a mental hospital, had difficulty getting the telephone connection to London. (*Frustriert*) he shouted to the operator, "Young lady, do you know who I am?" (*Ungerührt*) the operator replied, "no sir, but I know where you are."

LEVEL II **LEVEL II : Tipps für Kenner**

---

3. Die Verben der Sinneswahrnehmung

> *see, hear, watch, observe, find, feel*

Nach diesen Verben steht entweder Partizip oder Infinitiv ohne großen Bedeutungsunterschied.

18

Verb + Partizip	Verb + Objekt + Infinitiv
I saw a burglar *climbing* through the window.	I *saw* a burglar *climb* through the window.
Wahrnehmung, *wie* etwas geschieht: häufig zur Betonung des Ablaufs eines Vorgangs.	Wahrnehmung, *dass* etwas geschieht: vor allem bei abgeschlossenen Ereignissen kurzer Dauer.

---

4. Present oder Past Participle nach Verben der Ruhe und Bewegung

> *arrive, come, get, go, leave, lie, remain, return, sit, stand, wait*

Present Participle für zwei gleichzeitige Handlungen	Past Participle für Ergebnis einer vorausgehenden Situation
He *stood waiting* for the rain to stop. Er saß da *und* wartete: deutsch oft durch "und" verbunden.	He *stood shocked* by the explosion in the middle of the road. Er stand schockiert da … : deutsch oft ebenfalls ein Partizip Perfekt.
They *came running* up to us. Sie kamen angelaufen.	They *arrived exhausted* by the long trip. Sie kamen erschöpft … an.

Time for a SMILE

Two business partners decided to *go fishing* together. *Sitting* on the bank *waiting* for a nibble one suddenly turned to the other. "I think I forgot to close the office safe!"

"Don't worry," said his partner, "after all, we're both here."

Die Partizipien

SPRACHFALLEN für Deutsche

Interpretationsprobleme

Problem 1:

Wrong

Asking what he thought about Heaven and Hell, Mark Twain replied, "I don't want to express an opinion *because having* friends in both places."

Right

Asked what he thought about Heaven and Hell, Mark Twain replied, "I don't want to express an opinion *having* friends in both places."

1. *Asked:* Past Participle, da passiver Sinn: Mark Twain hat nicht gefragt, *er wurde gefragt.*
2. *Having:* Present Participle verkürzt einen Nebensatz des Grundes *"because he had friends ..."* (5.e). Die Konjunktion *because* muss wegfallen.

Problem 2:

Oft muss man die Bedeutung der Partizipialsätze und die richtige Zeitstufe aus dem Kontext erschließen.

Having no idea whether they had enough money, they entered the shop.	*Although they had* no idea whether they had enough money, they entered the shop.

Time for a SMILE

"My daughter is very clever. She speaks three languages and now she's learning algebra. Sally, tell Mrs Thomas what the word for 'Hello' is in algebra."

Merlins **Reifeprüfung**

E. **Find the meaning of Participle sentences from the context. You have the choice between:**

> *and, as soon as, because, if, while*

1. He welcomed us, politely *bowing* to all of us.
   → He welcomed us _____ bowed politely to all of us.
2. *Entering* her bedroom she turned on the lights.
   → _____ she entered her bedroom she turned on the lights.
3. He took no notice of us, *being* interested in what was happening at the other side of the street.
   → He took no notice of us, _____ he was interested in what was happening at the other side of the street.

F. **Put the verbs in the brackets into the correct form.**

1. Tom: I can't believe John is in hospital. I've just seen him (*hug*) and (*kiss*) a beautiful young blond girl in a restaurant.
   Tim: So did his wife.
2. To get something (*do*) a committee should consist of no more than three men, two of whom are absent.
3. The newly elected member of Parliament, nervously (*search*) for the manuscript for his speech, became even more nervous when (*ask*) by the speaker: "Are you ready or shall we let them enjoy themselves a bit longer?"

G. **Make your choice.**

1. The telephone will ring when you are having a shower. You will reach it just in time to hear the click of the caller _____ up.
   a. hang   **b.** hanging   **c.** hung
2. Since the introduction of computers at the workplace, I'm now the second smartest thing _____ at my desk.
   a. sat   **b.** being sat   **c.** sitting
3. It's nice of you, doctor, _____ my wife away for a rest. Heaven knows, I need it.
   a. sent   **b.** to send   **c.** sending

Die Partizipien

Merlin's saga

Worn out after a *particularly* bad week in Heidelmountain, Merlin was thinking how his life in the twenty-first century should go on. Merlin was walking beside the beautiful river Neckar. He sat down and rested **dangling** his feet in the warm water. (There's an atomic power station upstream). And who should come **jogging** along the path but Bob, one of the authors of our friendly masterpiece. **Shattered** after his twenty kilometre run Bob was glad to sit next to the weary wizard. "You're certainly very active for an old *civil servant*," Merlin greeted Bob, **moving** over to make space for him. "Yes, I'm into all that wellness, you know. We only have one life and that's short enough." **Amused** by Bob's comment, Merlin laughed. "You only have one short life. It's different for me **being** an *ancient* wizard. And this wizard needs a break. I'm tired out with all these *rude* fellows around here **draining** the life energy out of my body." Bob watched Merlin **wringing** his hands. It was true. The whitebeard was really looking a bit grey around the face. "Listen," said Bob, **putting** his brown healthy hand upon Merlin's *fragile* shoulder. "I know a great little holiday camp **located** on a small island called Majorca. You can train your body and I do believe they work with *potions* and oils there. You'll feel completely at home." **Motivated** by Bob's suggestion, Merlin *ripped off* his clothes and sprang into the river. A whistle blew on the bridge. **Looking** up, Bob saw the green uniform.

erschöpft; besonders

baumeln

absolut erledigt

Beamter

amüsiert

uralt
rüde

zerbrechlich

Trank

herunterreißen

18

Der bestimmte Artikel – The Definite Article

CHECK your Definite Articles

Spot the mistake

a. The university is an institution for the postponement of experience.

b. Amusement is happiness of those who cannot think.

c. What sort of people go to the Heaven? – Dead ones.

d. The most young blokes stop looking for work the moment they get a job.

e. The most dangerous part of our expedition to Africa was crossing the Piccadilly Circus. (JOSEPH THOMSON)

Tick them off

Right Wrong

a. The art of medicine consists in amusing the patient while the nature cures the disease.

b. My wife is the most wonderful woman in the world, and that's not just my opinion – it's hers.

c. Most women are not as young as they are painted.

d. The dinner last night was excellent.

e. The dinner is ready. Come in at once.

Time for a SMILE

Three Scotsmen were visiting London and on Sunday they went *to church.* As the collection plate moved closer and closer, they became more and more worried. Just before the plate reached them, one of the Scotsmen fainted and the other two carried him out of *the church.*

Der bestimmte Artikel

LEVEL I : Das Einmaleins des bestimmten Artikels

19

Globalregeln

Sind Nomen (also Personen, Dinge, Ideen, Institutionen etc.) *näher bestimmt oder bereits erwähnt*, steht der bestimmte Artikel *the.*	Nomen stehen ohne bestimmten Artikel, wenn sie *im allgemeinen Sinn* verwendet werden, das heißt nicht näher bestimmt sind.

Detailregeln

Näher bestimmt: *the*	Verallgemeinert: kein Artikel

1. Abstrakte Begriffe wie *art, life, death, love, nature, fear, hatred, poverty, wealth, happiness, luck, history, politics, science, society*

Sociology is *the science* with the greatest number of methods and the least results.	*Science* is the orderly arrangement of what, at the moment, seems to be the facts.
Tact is the art of saying nothing when there is nothing to say.	*Life* is too short to learn German.

2. Namen von Stoffen wie *alcohol, honey, silver* und Gattungsnamen im Plural wie *bees, cows, politicians, teachers*

Mother: *The Geography teacher* says Johnny should have an encyclopedia. Father: Nonsense. Let him walk to school like I did.	*Teachers* are persons who speak in somebody else's sleep. *Politicians* are persons with whose politics we don't agree. If we agree with them, they are *statesmen*.

3. Namen von Festen, Monaten, Tagen, Mahlzeiten, Schulfächern

"My daughter gets married on *the first Saturday* in May." "How do you feel about it?" "Well, I'm losing a daughter but I am gaining a telephone!"	Bisexuality immediately doubles your chances for a date on *Saturday*. (WOODY ALLEN)

4. Namen und Verwandtschaftsbezeichnungen

Familiennamen im Plural stehen mit bestimmtem Artikel

"I've come to tune your piano, sir." – "I always do that myself. Who asked you to come?" – *"The Joneses*, next door, sir."

Namen im Singular und wie Namen gebrauchte Verwandt-schaftsbezeichnungen stehen ohne Artikel.

"Where are the Himalayas, Dad?" asked *little Johnny*.
"Ask *Mother*," replied his father. "She always puts everything away."

19

5. Geographische Namen und Ländernamen

Die Ländernamen im Plural, Gebirge (*the Himalayas, the Alps*), Flüsse (*the Thames*), Meere, Meeresteile (*the Channel*)

The West of *the United States* is a place where men are men. In Soho you're never sure.

Ländernamen im Singular, ein-zelne Berge (*Ben Nevis*), Seen (*Lake Windermere*)
Ausnahme: *the Zugspitze*

Tom: I flew from *Switzerland* to *Turkey* last summer.
Tim: So did I. Doesn't it make your arms tired?

6. Namen von Straßen, Plätzen, Parks etc.

Mit Artikel: Namen mit einer *of*-Ergänzung, die bei bekannten Sehenswürdigkeiten wegfallen kann.
the Tower (of London)
the Houses (of Parliament)

Meist ohne Artikel:
Piccadilly Circus
Oxford Street
Trafalgar Square
Hyde Park
Aber: *the High Street*
the King's Road

Merke: Substantivierte Adjektive stehen mit Artikel:

✪ bestimmter Artikel für Plural: *the poor, the rich*
✪ unbestimmter Artikel für Singular: *a poor man, a poor woman*

Merlins **Merlins Zwischenprüfung**

19

A. You decide! With or without "the"?

1. Don't you love ___ nature, despite what it did to you?

2. There are worse things in ___ life than ___ death. Have you ever spent an evening with an insurance salesman?
   (WOODY ALLEN)

3. "I hear you are going into ___ hospital next week for a brain operation. The doctors hope to give you one."
   "Yes, I believe it's ___ hospital where you got yours."

B. Translate the German in the brackets.

1. (*Die Liebe*) is only a dirty trick played on us by (*die Evolution*) to achieve the continuation of the species.

2. (*Der Tod*) means stopping sinning suddenly.

3. Meetings: All important decisions will be made in the last five minutes (*vor dem Mittagessen*) or the end of the day.

4. (*Die Politik*) we are experiencing at the moment will destroy Europe.

C. Spot the mistakes.

1. You can always tell when there is a national catastrophe in United States. President puts black armbands around his golf clubs.

2. Believe it or not. The alcohol makes you fat.

3. In Soviet Union a writer who is critical is sent to a lunatic asylum. In USA he is taken to a talk show.

LEVEL II : Tipps für Kenner

Globalregeln

Sind Verkehrsmittel und Gebäude näher bestimmt beziehungsweise sind sie nur Ortsangabe, gebraucht man *the*.

Wird der Zweck oder die Funktion von Gebäuden und Verkehrsmitteln betont, steht kein Artikel.

7. Institutionen und Gebäude:
school, college, university, hospital, prison, church

All the great economic ills the world has known this century can be directly traced back to *the London School of Economics.* (N. M. PERRERA).

"When do you like *school* best?"
"When it's closed down."

A pedestrian is a father with a car and whose son is home from *college.*

8. Verkehrsmittel:
bus, car, train, plane, ship

The bus was so crowded that even the school kids didn't get seats.

I flew over *on Concorde. The plane* is so fast it gives you an extra couple of hours to look for your luggage. (BOB HOPE)

Typisch Englisch

9. Stellung des Artikels in Verbindung mit
all, both, double, half, twice, three times ... + Nomen

An expert is a man who has made *all the mistakes* that can be made, in a narrow field. (NIELS BOHR)
German companies design a new machine and within three months the Russians have invented it, and a month later the Japanese are making it for *half the price.*

✪ Der Artikel steht anders als im Deutschen *nach* der Mengenangabe.

Der bestimmte Artikel

---

10. Scheinbar Widersprüchliches

in the fall	in autumn
the Gold Coast, the White House,	Long Island, Latin America,
the Empire State Building	northern Italy
the UN, the EU	UNO, NATO
the Prince of Wales	Charles, Prince of Wales

SPRACHFALLEN für Deutsche

	Falsch	Richtig
1. Die meisten Hunde sind klug.	*The most dogs are clever.*	*Most* dogs are clever.
2. Der arme Tom!	*The poor Tom!*	*Poor* Tom!
3. Das menschliche Leben ist kurz.	*The human life is short.*	*Human life* is short.
4. Das Leben auf dieser Erde ist kurz.	*The life on our planet is short.*	*Life* on our planet is short.
5. Er kommt aus der Türkei.	*He comes from the Turkey.*	He comes *from Turkey.*
6. Die Erforschung des Weltraums.	*The exploration of the space.*	The exploration *of space.*

✪ Zu 1: *the most* nur vor Superlativen.

✪ Zu 2: Namen ohne Artikel, auch mit vorangestelltem Adjektiv

✪ Zu 3, 4: Abstrakta ohne Artikel, wenn allgemein gebraucht

✪ Zu 5: Ländernamen und Städtenamen im Singular ohne Artikel, aber: *the Hague*

✪ Zu 6: Einzigartiges wie *the Universe* oder *the moon* steht gewöhnlich mit Artikel. Man merke als Ausnahme *space* = Weltraum.

Merlins **Reifeprüfung**

D. Make your choice.

1. _____ is the ability to give directions without taking your hands out of your pockets.
   a. The clarity   **b.** Clarity

2. _____ of space is expected to cost us billions of dollars.
   a. Exploration   **b.** The exploration

3. A famous footballer once said that _____ the people on unemployment are lazy.
   a. the most of   **b.** most of

E. Right or wrong?

1. Specialists that I work with are people who know everything about nothing and nothing about anything else.

2. Ron: Are you trying to make a fool of me?
   Bob: I never interfere with the nature.

3. The chairman of the Board of Directors once visited one of his directors in the hospital. "Bob," he said, "the Board of Directors wishes you a speedy recovery – and it was a majority decision of seven to five."

F. Translate the German in the brackets.

1. "What did you do (*in der Schule*) today?"
   "Oh," he answers, "in chemistry we made explosives."
   "And what are you doing at school tomorrow?"
   Thereupon (*der kleine Joe*) asks: "At which school?"

2. When I was young I thought money was (*das Wichtigste*) (*im Leben*). Now that I am old, I know that it is. (OSCAR WILDE)

3. (*Der kleine Billy*) brought a note home (*aus der Schule*). His dad read it and announced to his wife: "They want a written excuse for his presence."

Der bestimmte Artikel

Merlin's saga

19

We wouldn't say that Merlin was anti-social exactly, but let's say he doesn't understand **the** rules of *behaviour*, **the** etiquette of the 21st century. (Who does by the way?) The background is as follows: Merlin had to get around a lot. He could go on foot but it was taking too long, so he decided to go **by car**. But that meant he had to buy a car. And he did just that. That's where **the** problems started. Our *weary* hero had to visit some *needy* and depressed people in Heidelmountain. He parked **the** car. He gave his *consultation* and advice with **the** usual little bit of magic built in and went back to his car. And what or who did he see? A man in a blue uniform sticking **the** second *parking fine* of the day onto Merlin's *windscreen*. The old wizard's white face turned red.

"Hey, that's **the** *rudest* thing I've ever seen. What's the reason for that?"

"You're parking here and you don't have **the** *permit* to do so."

"But I'm here doing good *deeds* for your fellow men."

"I don't care if you're *cloning* **the** whole human race. You have not put **the** Westtown ticket in **the** window of your car. I can't help **the** rules. I'm just a *civil servant* doing my *duty*. And you are a criminal."

The last word was a sort of croaking *noise* as the frog with a ticket machine was last seen *hopping* away along the road (in what seemed to be a blue uniform).

	Verhalten
	matt; bedürftig
	Beratung
	Strafzettel
	Windschutz-scheibe
	unverschämteste
	Erlaubnis
	Taten
	klonen
	Beamter
	Pflicht
	Geräusch
	hoppeln

CHECK your Indefinite Article

Spot the mistake

a. A filing cabinet is an useful container where things can be lost alphabetically.

b. Ronny was trying to explain to Annette all about nuclear plants. After an half hour she said, "Yes, but what colour are the petals?"

c. A diplomat is a man who can tell you to go to hell in a such way that you actually look forward to the trip.

d. You are alcoholic if you drink more than your doctor.

Tick them off

Right Wrong

a. My boss is a conservative. He thinks that nothing should be done for the first time.

b. My father is teacher. He talks in his pupils' sleep.

c. You're not really a such bad person – until people get to know you better.

d. What a weather! It's raining cats and dogs.

e. He was a great patriot, an humanitarian, a loyal friend – provided of course he really is dead. (VOLTAIRE)

Time for a SMILE

The personnel manager called John into the office and said, "It hasn't escaped me that every time Liverpool is playing at home you ask permission to go and visit your grandmother who's seriously ill." "What *an* incredible coincidence," exclaimed John. "You don't think, by any chance, she's faking it?"

Der unbestimmte Artikel

LEVEL I : Das Einmaleins des unbestimmten Artikels

Form und Aussprache

1. Vor Konsonant steht *a*; vor Vokal steht *an*.	What's the difference between *a doctor* and *an architect*? – Well, a doctor can bury his failures.
2. Diese Regel gilt für Adjektive und Nomen.	Chess is *an intelligent game* invented by princes to save money.
3. Vor konsonantischem *u [j]* wie in *Europe* oder *united* steht *a*; vor stummem *h* wie in *honest* oder *hour* steht *an*.	*A university* is *an institution* for the postponement of experience. Vergleiche: A bank is a place where they lend you *an umbrella* in fair weather and ask for it back when it begins to rain. *An honest politician* is one who, when he is bought, will stay bought.

Gebrauch

Der unbestimmte Artikel ordnet Menschen einer Gruppe oder einem Menschentypen zu. Deshalb steht er zur Angabe

4. von Beruf und Hobby	*A statesman is a politician* who didn't get caught.
5. der Nationalität und Religion	A xenophobe is *a German* at home.
6. der politischen Partei	A *liberal* is a *conservative* who has been arrested.
7. des Typs und Charakters	Tim is *a vegetarian*. He eats vegetables not because he loves animals, but because he hates plants.

Merlins Zwischenprüfung

A. Spot the mistakes.

1. Motivation is usually the promise of either a bonus, a assigned parking space or a office with a window.

20

2. You seem to know more and more about less and less, Bob: you're becoming expert.

3. He hasn't a enemy in this world and none of his friends like him either.

B. Is it *a, an, the* or no Article?

1. "I wish you a happy birthday. May you live to be _____ hundred and then decide if you want to go on."

2. Psychiatrist: How long have you believed in _____ reincarnation?
   Patient: Ever since I was _____ frog.

3. The upstairs tenant called to the downstairs tenant:
   "Must you play _____ trumpet all day long? If you don't stop I'll go crazy!" – "I'm afraid it's too late," was the reply. "I stopped _____ hour ago."

C. Which is correct?

1. Ron: I'd like to know how long *the / a* human being is able to live without a brain.
   Anne: How old are you?

2. Bob: If only I knew whether to be —- / *a* painter or —- / *a* poet.
   Ron: I think you should be ___ / *a* poet.
   Bob: You mean you've read one of my poems?
   René: No, but I've seen one of your paintings.

3. Ron: How do you like the change from being a salesman to *a* / —- teacher?
   Bob: Fine. The pay is regular and the hours are good. But what I like most is that the pupil is always wrong.

4. A manager is *an / a* ulcer with authority.

Der unbestimmte Artikel

LEVEL II : Tipps für Kenner

8. Nach Maß- und Zeitangaben steht der unbestimmte Artikel (deutsch: *pro, je*):

> one dollar *an* hour, three pence *a* kilo,
> fifty miles *an* hour, five euros *a* meter
> three times *a* day, once *a* week, twice *a* year,

A young man asked an experienced marketing consultant. "Tell me, can I earn *a million dollars a year* by selling flour?" – "Of course," replied the consultant, "all you need to do is buy a million bags of flour *at a dollar a kilo* and sell them for a *dollar a pound*!"

9. Der unbestimmte (wie auch der bestimmte) Artikel steht in der Regel vor Adjektiv und Nomen. Ausnahmen:

> *half a* bottle, *such a* day, for *quite a* while

Tony is *such a* bore, even my legs fall asleep when he talks.

SPRACHFALLEN für Deutsche

	Falsch	Richtig
1. mit einem Wort	*in one word*	in *a* word
2. auf einen Blick	*at one glance*	at *a* glance
3. in der Regel	*as the rule*	as *a* rule
4. Platz nehmen	*take place*	take *a* seat
5. zu Ende gehen	*come to end*	come to *an* end
6. Was für ein Unsinn!	*What a nonsense!*	What nonsense!
7. Was für ein Wetter!	*What a weather!*	What weather!
8. Wie schade!	*What pity!*	What *a* pity!

✪ Zu 1–8: Es handelt sich hier vorwiegend um Redewendungen, die keiner Regel folgen.

✪ Zu 1,2: Der unbestimmte Artikel wird häufig anstelle des Zahlworts *one* verwendet: *a hundred people, a million dollars.*

✪ Zu 6–8: Vor Dingen, die man nicht zählen kann (*uncountables*) steht kein Artikel. Aber: *What a pity! What a shame!*

Merlins **Reifeprüfung**

D. Complete the exclamations with *an* or *a* where necessary.

1. What ....day!
2. What .... fool you are!
3. What .... weather!
4. What ...... sad news!

5. What ...... awful experience!
6. What ...... interesting information
7. What .... intelligent manager!
8. What ..... nonsense!

20

E. Spot the mistakes again.

1. Amy Fernandez works as receptionist at Low Valley Copiers.
2. She is a happy girl. What a fun her life could be if she didn't have to work.
3. After work she goes to the Irish pub where she drinks a half bottle of wine.
4. Anyway, she has enough money. She earns fifty thousand euros the year.

F. Now we'll mix it a bit. Fill in the correct Articles (*a, an, the*), but only if necessary.

David Jones is (1) _____ Englishman and (2) _____ engineer by profession. I met him during our last term (3) _____ university and we soon became close friends. (4) _____ life with him was not easy in those days. He had to work as (5) _____ waiter at the restaurant opposite (6) _____ university during his holidays.

David was very interested in topics like (7) _____ technical progress and its effects (8) _____ society. His motto was "(9) _____ Times have changed and man must change with them. In (10) _____ word we must be flexible."

G. Fit in the words in the brackets.

1. In Glasgow, Scotland: A wife arrives home from shopping and puts six bottles of whiskey and (*half / loaf / bread*) on the table. Her husband saw this and shouted at her angrily, "Why in the Lord's name did you bring all that bread home?"
2. Excuse for not coming to the office on a Friday: My aunt hid (*quite / sum / large*) of money before she died. My lawyer arranged a séance with a medium to find where it's hidden.

Der unbestimmte Artikel

Merlin's saga

We all know the *famous* phrase "it's been one of those days." Everything that can go wrong goes wrong. And Saturday was **a** day like that for Merlin. By now he had been living in the 21st century for about six months. It was Merlin's feeling that in his role as **a** wizard he should *at least* live in an apartment like a "civilized" *citizen*. Besides, not all his clients liked to visit him in **a** cave – too cold, too windy.

On this *particular* Saturday Merlin went to his fridge, **an** old red Coca Cola fridge he had found on the roadside on what the locals call "*Rubbish*" day. You know **a** German is **a** very practical person, so it had very quickly become **a** tradition in Germania to have **a** special day when you could throw out the things you don't want. Anyhow, once **a** *quarter* there were *piles* of furniture all over the place. As we were saying, he went to his fridge to get some of that very tasty colourless *liquid* which **a** Russian friend had given him as **a** present. He *gripped* the bottle which slipped easily through his fingers and fell to the floor. "Damn it. That was half **a** bottle and it's all *wasted*. Where's my wand?" Merlin limped off. He *stomped* hard straight onto **a** piece of broken glass. "Ouuuch!" he *screeched*. (Even wizards feel *pain*, you know). **A** knock at the door. It was Bob. "My God, what **a** *mess*! There's blood everywhere." At **a** glance Bob's *superior* intelligence took in the scene. "If you can't heal yourself we will have to get you to **a** hospital. You can get some *stitches* in that *wound*." Merlin was very *annoyed*. "What **a** waste of time. I'll probably have to sit around waiting for **an** hour or more. What did I do to *deserve* this?" Bob's nose was active. "Merlin, I think I can smell alcohol. What on earth have you been doing?" "**A** turbo charge. Nothing more than **a** short turbo charge." Merlin's white beard turned bright red.

berühmt

wenigstens
Bürger

speziellen

Sperrmüll

Quartal; Haufen

Flüssigkeit
greifen

vergeudet
stampfen
schreien
Schmerz
Durcheinander
überlegen

Stiche
Wunde; verärgert

verdienen

Adjektiv und Adverb –
Adjective and Adverb

CHECK your Adjectives and Adverbs

 Spot the mistake

a. Peter can run more fast than me.
b. It was a bad accident and some people were bad injured.
c. This is a dangerous road, you should drive more careful.
d. Tom plays tennis well, but he doesn't always play fairly.
e. Where is the next taxi stand, please?

 Tick them off

Right Wrong

a. A man who looks you *straight* in the eye and adds a *firm* handshake is hiding something.

b. It's *hard* to feel fit as a fiddle when you're shaped like a cello.

c. Comics are *fast* reading for the *slowly* thinking.

d. The thief ran *always faster.*

Time for a SMILE

It's *easy* to be a humorist when you have the whole government working for you.
(WILL ROGERS)

151

LEVEL I : Das Einmaleins von Adjektiv und Adverb[1]

21

Der Unterschied zwischen Adjektiv und Adverb

Er ist *langsam*.	He is *slow*.
Er isst *langsam*.	He eats *slowly*.

Das Problem: die Engländer unterscheiden – wir nicht.

Das Adjektiv	Das Adverb

1. Es drückt Eigenschaften von Substantiven aus. Es steht
  a. *vor* dem Substantiv oder
  b. *nach* dem Verb als Ergänzung. *It smells good.*
	3. Es bestimmt
	  a. Verben (wie geschieht es?)
	  b. Adjektive und Adverbien (wie sehr? / wie viel?)

2. Manche Adjektive kann man als Substantiv gebrauchen.
  a. im Plural ohne *-s*
  b. im Singular durch Zusatz von *person, man, woman, one* Ausnahmen: *the whites, the blacks, the Liberals ...*
	4. a. Man bildet die meisten Adverbien durch Anhängen von *ly* an das Adjektiv.
	  b. Rechtschreibung:
	  happ*y* ➜ happil*y*: *y* ➜ *i*
	  tru*e* ➜ tru*ly*: End-*e* fällt weg
	  typ*ical* ➜ typ*ically*:
	  ical ➜ *ically*

✪ Zu 1 a: A *smart* husband thinks twice before he says nothing.

✪ Zu 1 b: The only time a husband is *right* is when he is *wrong*.

✪ Zu 2 a: Irish paradox: "It's a funny thing, that *the poor*, who need money the most, are always the ones who never seem to have it."

✪ Zu 2 b: "Mike," Bridget asked, "What would you do if you found £100?" "Well, it all depends," said Mike, "who had lost it. If it was a *poor person*, I'd certainly return it."

✪ Zu 3 a, 4 b: My husband and I had lived *happily* for many years – then we met.

✪ Zu 3 b, 4 a: Long-term weather forecast: The weather for this summer will be *partly cloudy, partly sunny, partly accurate*.

---

1 Es geht in diesem Kapitel vor allem um das Adverb der Art und Weise.

Merlins *Merlins* Zwischenprüfung 1

A. Is it late or lately, quick or quickly?

1. Angry boss: Why are you (*verspätet*) again this morning?
   Secretary: I overslept.
   Boss: You mean you sleep at home as well?

2. "Why, McGregor," said the doctor. "You have lost your stutter!"
   "Yes," said McGregor, "I've been telephoning Australia (*in letzter Zeit*)."

3. Nothing worth learning is learned (*schnell*), except parachuting.

B. Spot the mistake.

1. Okay, I'm very angry. I'll come straightly to the point.

2. Advertising may be described as the science of arresting the human intelligence longly enough to get money from it.

3. Shoemaker drove much too rapid and was almost killed in a crash.

C. It's your choice.

1. When I take a long time – I'm *slow / slowly*.
   When my boss takes a long time – he's *thorough / thoroughly*.

2. First secretary: "What do you think of our new boss?"
   Second secretary: "He dresses *smart / smartly*."
   First secretary: "And *quick / quickly* too!"

3. People who cough *loudly / loud* never go to the doctor – they go to the theatre or a concert.

Adjektiv und Adverb

Die Steigerung der meisten Adjektive und Adverbien

Adjektive	Adverbien
5. Mehrsilbige Adjektive *more* interesting *most* interesting	6. Adverbien auf *-ly* *more* slowly *most* slowly

Ausnahmen

7. Einsilbige Adjektive long, long*er*, long*est* great, great*er*, great*est* far, farth*er*, farth*est* 8. Einige zweisilbige Adjektive auf *-er, -le, -ow, -y* clev*er*, cleve*rer*, cleve*rest* sim*ple*, simp*ler*, simp*lest* eas*y*, eas*ier*, eas*iest* a*ble*, ab*ler*, ab*lest* narr*ow*, narr*ower*, narr*owest*	9. Adverb und Adjektiv mit gleicher Form fast, fast*er*, fast*est* long, long*er*, long*est* loud, loud*er*, loud*est* hard, hard*er*, hard*est* Ebenso die Gegensatzpaare high – low; far – near early – late – soon

10. Unregelmäßige Steigerung

a. Adjektive	b. Adverbien
gut, besser, am besten	
good, better, best	well, better, best

Anne: Am I the only girl you have kissed?
Bill: Of course, and by far the *best*-looking.

schlecht, schlechter, am schlechtesten	
bad, worse, worst	badly, worse, worst

Murphy's Law:
Anything that begins *well*, ends *badly*.
Anything that begins *badly*, ends *worse*.

klein, kleiner, am kleinsten – wenig, weniger, am wenigsten	
little, smaller, smallest	little, less, least

Several excuses are always *less* convincing than one excuse.

Merlins **Merlins Zwischenprüfung 2**

D. Put the word in the brackets into the correct form.

1. Anne: I've just jogged twenty kilometres.
   Ron: My God, that's the *(far)* you've ever run.

2. John: That's the *(easy)* exam I've ever done.

3. Since he has been eating animal fat his arteries have become *(narrow)* and *(narrow)*.

E. Make your choice.

1. An intellectual is a man who has found something _____ than women.
   a. more interesting   **b.** interestinger

2. Drive _____ or we'll be killed.
   a. slowlier   **b.** more slowly

3. He must be a _____ educated person or he wouldn't know all the answers.
   a. high-   **b.** highly-

F. Translate the German.

1. A watch is something a woman looks at to see how *(spät)* she is.

2. It must have been *(leicht)* to pass your motor-bike test than it was in my day. I failed it three times.

3. School children have a *(faszinierenderes)* life than we had. They can travel everywhere they want.

LEVEL II : Tipps für Kenner

Zwei besondere Steigerungsformen

11. Allmähliche Steigerung

immer größer   bigger *and* bigger

An expert is a man who learns *more and more* about *less and less*.

12. Proportionale Steigerung

je größer, *desto* besser   *the* bigger, *the* better

Fun and sex are like a life insurance: *the older* you get, *the more* it costs.
The trouble with the future is that it's getting *closer and closer*.

Adjektiv und Adverb in Vergleichen

13. Gleichheit

 =

Tim is as tall *as* Tom.
Tim works *as* fast *as* Tom.

A man is *as old as* the woman he feels.

14. Ungleichheit

Tim is *not as / so* tall *as* Tom.
Tim *doesn't* work *as* well *as* Tom.
Tim is small*er than* Tom.
Tim works *more* slowly *than* Tom.
Tom works fast*er than* Tim.

You know that you are getting old when the candles cost *more than* the cake.
Women are *wiser than* men because they know less and understand more.

○ Für Adjektiv und Adverb werden also dieselben Strukturen verwendet. Gleichheit: *as .... as;* Ungleichheit: *not so ... as / smaller ... than / more ... than*

Adjektiv oder Adverb nach bestimmten Verben

15. Adjektiv	16. Adverb
The milk *tastes sour*.	He *tasted* the soup *carefully*.
The cake *looks delicious*.	He looked *hungrily* at the cake.
The food *smells* strange.	He *smelled* the food suspiciously.

21

✪ Zu 15: Nach den Verben *taste*: schmecken, *smell*: riechen, *look*: aussehen und *sound*: klingen steht Adjektiv, wenn eine Eigenschaft oder Qualität beschrieben wird. Man könnte diese Verben durch eine Form von *to be* ersetzen.

✪ Zu 16: Wenn diese Verben eine Tätigkeit ausdrücken, steht Adverb. Sie ändern dabei ihre Bedeutung: *smell*: beriechen, *taste*: kosten, abschmecken; *look:* ansehen.

Leicht zu verwechselnde Doppelformen

17. Adjektive

old	older	oldest	the oldest town	Alter
	elder	eldest	my eldest son	familiäre Beziehung
late	later	latest	the latest news	Zeitrelation
	latter	last	letzterer	Reihenfolge
near	nearer	nearest	the nearest town	Entfernung
		next	the next station	Reihenfolge

interesting	interessant
interested in	interessiert an
embarrassing	peinlich, unangenehm
embarrassed	verlegen
depressing	deprimierend
depressed	deprimiert

Time for a SMILE

"Why are you looking so *depressed*?" – "I've just been to the doctor and he told me I would have to take a pill every day for the rest of my life." – "Why is that so *depressing*?" – "He only gave me twenty-five pills."

21

<table>
<tr><td colspan="3" align="center">18. Adverbien mit zwei Formen</td></tr>
<tr><td>fair</td><td>fair</td><td>They are all very fair sportsmen.</td></tr>
<tr><td>fairly</td><td>ziemlich</td><td>I know the rugby team fairly well.</td></tr>
<tr><td>hard</td><td>hart</td><td>He thinks he's a hard worker.</td></tr>
<tr><td>hardly</td><td>kaum</td><td>But he has hardly done anything so far.</td></tr>
<tr><td>near</td><td>nah</td><td>The girl went too near to the river and</td></tr>
<tr><td>nearly</td><td>beinah</td><td>nearly fell into the water.</td></tr>
</table>

SPRACHFALLEN  für Deutsche

	Falsch	Richtig
1. Der Dieb rannte *immer schneller*.	*The thief ran always faster.*	The thief ran *faster and faster*.
2. Er lächelte *freundlich*.	*He smiled friendlily.*	He smiled *in a friendly way*.
3. Haben Sie unser *letztes* Buch gelesen?	*Have you read our last book?*	Have you read our *latest* book?
4. My *late* husband.	*Mein verspäteter Mann.*	Mein *verstorbener* Mann.
5. This dog is *most dangerous*.	*Dieser Hund ist der gefährlichste.*	Dieser Hund ist *äußerst gefährlich*.

✪ Zu 1: Ein typischer Fehler, siehe Level II: 11.

✪ Zu 2: Adjektive auf *-ly* erhalten kein zweites *-ly*. Man umschreibt: in a friendly way / manner / style. So auch Adjektive wie *difficult*, die kein Adverb auf *-ly* bilden.

✪ Zu 3: last: das Letzte in einer Reihenfolge, siehe auch Level II: 17.

Merlins **Reifeprüfung**

G. Make your choice.

1. An elderly businessman had problems with his sex life. "You've been working *too hard / hardly*. Get some exercise," his doctor advised. "Try riding a bike a few miles every day."
   Two days later the doctor received a phone-call from the man.
   "How are you this morning? Has your sex life improved?" he asked.
   "How would I know? I *hardly / hard* know where home is. I'm at least fifty miles away," was the angry reply.

2. "I was extremely *embarrassed / embarrassing* yesterday. I called my wife Sue."
   "What's *embarrassing / embarrassed* about that?"
   "Her name's Anne."

3. My *newest / latest* invention is an automatic pancake. You put pop-corn in the dough so that it will turn over by itself.

4. Lizzie couldn't get a man however *hardly / hard* she tried. But one day a gypsy sold her a special Chinese love potion for fifty cents − and it worked. A week later she married the Chinese Ambassador.

5. Bob did well in his English test. He came *near / nearly* to the top.

H. Spot the mistake.

1. Anne: Nonsense! I can't really believe that you'll kill yourself if I refuse to go to bed with you. That's ridiculously.
   Ron: It's been my usual procedure until now. So don't provoke me.

2. Her hat is a creation that will never go out of style. It will look ridi-culously year after year.

3. The small company always got into more debts.

21

Merlin's saga

21

Bob and Ron, both felt very **warm** towards Merlin. He had been **really** helpful to them. He had shown Bob how to throw off his depression and had **quickly** *cured* Ron of his hypochondria. "Merlin's been looking rather **thin** and **ill lately**. Let's invite him for a special, healthy meal," suggested Bob. "I know the perfect place." (Bob always knows things like that as he spends most of his time eating healthy *bits and pieces*).

heilen

Zeug

One week later the three *sufferers* are sitting together in a Thai restaurant.

Leidende

B: I must say I would have preferred to have something French or Italian. I can **hardly** taste the *ingredients,* there is so much *hot spice* in the meal.

Zutaten
scharfe Gewürze

R: Bob, you're the biggest *moaner* I've ever met. The hot curry will clean out your **blocked-up** system.

Nörgler

M: The food does bite the inside of the mouth **aggressively**. It certainly contains *herbs* for losing one's extra weight.

Kräuter

B: Oh, that's news! That's really **interesting**. What sort of herbs are they?

M: They speed up your *metabolism* and so you burn up your calories **quickly**.

Stoffwechsel

B: That's **amazing**. Waiter, I say, waiter (Bob was getting **louder and louder**), could you bring me two portions of that curry potion? It tastes *lousy* but it *gets rid of* the pounds.

erstaunlich

miserabel;
loswerden

Bob leaned back with a **satisfied** smile on his face.

CHECK your Nouns

22

Spot the mistake

a. A man was found lying in a field with a knife sticking out of his back. The police suspects foul play.

b. The Red Indians are worried. The United States want to give the country back to them.

c. Journalists often have to take risks to get the informations they require.

d. Your presentation has been most entertaining. But are there some hard facts to follow?

e. Our President is a man of little words. Unfortunately he keeps repeating them.

Tick them off

Right Wrong

a. In Marseille the government is trying to stop gambling. Many officers are bankrupt.

b. Australia – a country where men are men, and sheep are nervous.

c. The news is never very good nowadays.

d. The room was so full of furnitures it was difficult to move.

e. Lots of persons confuse bad management with destiny.

Time for a SMILE

A man visited a large town in Australia and asked one of the locals:
"Does this town have *any* night life?"
"Yes," replied the local, "but she's ill today."

LEVEL I : Das Einmaleins der englischen Nomen

1. Männlich oder weiblich?

a. Es ist manchmal nicht leicht herauszufinden, von wem die Rede ist.

Zwitter: männlich und weiblich

Steward, Stewardess	flight attendant
Sekretär, Sekretärin	secretary
Lehrer, Lehrerin	teacher
Krankenschwester, Pfleger(in)	nurse

b. Im Zweifelsfalle kann man *man / woman* anhängen oder *male / female* oder *lady* vorausschicken.

Männlich	Weiblich
actor	actress
host	hostess
salesman	saleswoman
businessman	businesswoman
policeman	policewoman
male teacher	female teacher
doctor	lady doctor
male nurse	female nurse

2. Endungsloser und unregelmäßiger Plural

a. Der endungslose Plural einiger Nutztiere ist für Deutsche ungewohnt.

Schaf	sheep, two sheep	Lachs	salmon, two salmon
Fisch	fish, some fish	Forelle	trout, some trout

b. Wir merken uns noch einige unregelmäßige Pluralformen:

child, children	tooth, teeth	goose, geese
life, lives	mouse, mice	person, people
thief, thieves	shelf, shelves	woman, women

3. Tiere im Stall und auf der Speisekarte

Tier	Produkt	Tier	Produkt
cow	beef	sheep	mutton, lamb
calf	veal	pig	pork

4. Mengenadverbien vor Countables und Uncountables

22

✪ *Countable nouns* bezeichnen Dinge, die wir zählen, zum Beispiel Freunde, Leute.

✪ *Uncountable nouns* bezeichnen Dinge, die man nicht zählt, und Mengen, die man wiegt oder misst.

a. Zählbares – Countables

He has *a few* good ideas.	Er hat *ein paar* gute Ideen.
He only has *few* friends.	Er hat nur *wenige* Freunde.
Many people are illiterate.	*Viele* Menschen sind Analphabeten.

b. Nichtzählbares, -messbares und -wägbares – Uncountables

Have you got *a little* time for me?	Hast du *ein bisschen* Zeit für mich?
He got *little* attention.	Er bekam *wenig* Aufmerksamkeit.

c. Mengenadverbien, die vor Countables und Uncountables stehen

a lot of / lots of water / apples	viel Wasser / viele Äpfel
plenty of water / time / friends	viel Zeit / viele Freunde
some money / some problems	etwas Geld / einige Probleme
There isn't any grass / there aren't any trees there.	Da gibt es kein Grass / keine Bäume

✪ *Some* steht in bejahten Sätzen und in Fragen, auf die man eine positive Antwort erwartet.

✪ *Any* steht in der Regel in verneinten Sätzen, in Fragen und Bedingungssätzen.

Time for a SMILE

I asked her if she liked Le Corbusier and she replied, "I'd love *some* – with *a little* lemon juice in it, if you've got *any*."

Probleme mit Nomen

Merlins Zwischenprüfung

A. Make your choice.

1. Ron: Doctor, doctor, _____ my hair fell out while I was brushing it this morning. Have you got anything for it?
   Doc: Sure. Here's a box.
   a. many of   **b.** lots of

2. Bob: Now that you are married, may I give you _____ advice? Take out _____ insurance.
   Ron: But why? My wife isn't dangerous.
   a. any   **b.** some

3. We all know that a cat has nine _____ .
   a. lifes   **b.** lives

B. Translate the German in the brackets.

1. An Irishman was fishing in winter when he suddenly heard a voice from overhead. "There are no (*Fische*) under the ice!" the voice boomed. The Irishman dropped his rod in panic and asked in a trembling voice, "Is that you God?" – "No", thundered the voice, "I'm the manager of the ice rink!"

2. He ought to go to a dentist and have some (*Weisheitszähne*) put in.

3. A man's credit card was stolen, but he decided not to tell the police because the thief was spending (*weniger*) money than his wife did.

C. Which is correct?

1. Call a meeting at 4:30 p.m. on Friday and you'll get *few / little* opposition.

2. *Thiefs / Thieves* escaped with over 600,000 pounds in a robbery in Glasgow. The police are trying to work out a motive for the crime.

3. There's *many / a lot of pigs / pork* on that plate. It's too much to eat.

LEVEL II : Tipps für Kenner

5. Paarwörter und Sammelbegriffe

a. Paarwörter sind Pluralwörter

trousers	Hosen	How much *are these* trousers?
jeans	Jeans	Are *those* your jeans?
shorts	kurze Hosen	Shorts *don't* sell well in winter.
scales	Waage	These scales *cost* a fortune.
scissors	Schere	Where *are* my scissors?

✪ Spricht man von Stückzahlen, fügt man *pair* hinzu:
a pair of trousers, *two pairs of* scissors etc.

b. Sammelbegriffe im Singular

furniture	Möbel
information	Informationen
advice	Rat
jewellery	Schmuck

c. Sammelbegriffe im Plural

stairs	Treppe
wages	Lohn
surroundings	Umgebung
thanks	Dank

✪ Zu b: Das Verb steht im Singular. *This is* good advice.
Spricht man von Zahlen, fügt man *piece* hinzu:
an old piece of furniture, *two valuable pieces of* jewellery.

✪ Zu c: Das Verb steht im Plural:
The *wages* at VW *are* good. *Thanks are* due to our teacher.
Unserem Lehrer gebührt Dank.

Time for a SMILE

The sales manager of a large export firm received news one morning that one of his top salesmen had died in Milan. He immediately sent a fax to the Milan office: "Return samples by airmail and search the body for orders."

Probleme mit Nomen

6. Gruppenwörter

Substantive, die sich auf Gruppen von Menschen in einer Organisation beziehen, können entweder im Plural oder Singular stehen.

the government, the team, the police, the crew, the fire brigade

a. im Plural

The *team are* worn out.

b. im Singular

The *team is* notorious for fouling.

✪ Zu a: Die Betonung liegt hier auf den einzelnen Personen in der Gruppe.
✪ Zu b: Hier wird die Gruppe als eine Einheit betont.

SPRACHFALLEN für Deutsche

	Falsch	Richtig
1. Zehn Dollar sind zu viel.	*Ten dollars are too much.*	Ten dollars *is* too much.
2. Wir müssen noch drei Meilen gehen	*Another three miles are all we have to walk.*	Another three miles *is* all we have to walk.
3. Die Vereinigten Staaten haben einen neuen Präsidenten.	*The United States have a new President.*	The United States *has* a new President.
4. Zu viele Leute!	*Too many peoples!*	Too many *people*!
5. I like these chocolates.	*Ich mag diese Schokoladen.*	Ich mag diese *Pralinen*.

✪ Zu 1, 2: Nach Maßangaben steht das Verb im Singular.
✪ Zu 3: Sprachgebrauch: The United States *is* ...
  Aber: The United Nations *are* ...
✪ Zu 4: Ein häufiger Fehler der Deutschen! *Peoples* sind Völker.

Time for a SMILE

Bill Gates doesn't pay income tax any more. He just asks the *Government* what *they* need.

Merlins Reifeprüfung

D. Spot the mistakes.

1. The best advices I was ever given were on my twenty-first birthday when my father said, "son, here's a million dollars. Don't lose it." (Larry Niven)
2. Annette arrived in Hong Kong and she hated it. There were far too many peoples on the streets.
3. Communism: You have two cows; the government take both and sell you the milk.

22

E. Translate the German in the brackets.

1. Definition of a lecture: a means of transferring (*Informationen*) from the notes of the lecturer to the notes of the student without passing through the minds of either.
2. "Can you give me (*eine Schere*). I need to cut this bankcard up."
3. (*Die Polizei ist*) all under-equipped. Moreover, (*sie trägt keine*) weapons in the U.K.

F. Make your choice.

At Frank's flat. Silvia and Frank:

F: Hi, Silvia. I haven't seen you for ages.

S: So this is your new place. I must say it's in *a very nice surrounding / very nice surroundings*.

F: Yes, but it's very expensive here in Heidelberg. Two thousand euros *is / are* too much to pay.

S: I'm afraid that's the same for all of us. The local government *is / are* only interested in robbing the population to pay for stupid things that we all don't need.

F: You're right and my *wages are / wage is* simply too small to cover this rent and all the extra costs.

Merlin's saga

22

Merlin had just eaten a large plate of **pork**, which had been specially prepared for him by Ron at his apartment. It was Ron's idea to *feed* the wizard up a bit, to put some flesh on those old *bones*. Of course, Ron had **lots of** great ideas for food, but unfortunately there was very **little** time to cook properly.

hochpäppeln
Knochen

The wizard was *full up* and so was Ron. "I wouldn't want to get on the *scales* at the moment. I must weigh over a hundred kilos," said Ron angrily. "Ah, that is a difference between your time and mine," commented the whitebeard. "A thousand years ago we gave **thanks** for the meal we had on the table. Nowadays you *swallow indigestion* tablets to recover from it." – "Well, I certainly don't fit into this **pair of jeans**," moaned fat Ron. "Let's do something. Let's go to the cinema."

vollkommen satt
Waage

schlucken; Verdauung

Merlin hadn't had any *experience* of the cinema. "What's that?" he asked. Pulling his jacket on Ron explained that cinema was like a large crystal *screen* where you could see scenes from different places and times.

Erfahrung

Bildschirm

Merlin's eyes lit up. "Yes, I know what you mean. I used it myself fifteen hundred years ago. I called it my crystal ball. I could see what was happening everywhere." Ron informed him it was not quite the same thing.

The film was Harry Potter. Ron *insisted* that the **cast was** super good. Merlin was very quiet during the show. At the end he asked Ron to get him the address of the school of magic where Harry was studying. "Well, there you are," laughed Ron. "**Ten euros** for the tickets **wasn't** really too much to pay, was it?"

darauf bestehen;
Besetzung

Key to the Exercises

1. Der Imperativ – The Imperative

Spot the mistake

a. Seien Sie vorsichtig! — Be ~~you~~ careful!
b. Reden wir übers Geschäft. — Let's talk business, ~~will~~ *shall* we?
c. Entweder oder. — Take ~~you~~ it or leave it.
d. Sei immer ehrlich! — *Always* be ~~always~~ honest!

Tick them off

		Right	Wrong
a.	Sit down, please.	✗	
b.	Sit ~~you~~ down, will you.		✗
c.	Help yourself, please.	✗	
d.	Don't sit down on this chair!	✗	
e.	Don't sit ~~you~~ down on that chair!		✗
f.	Please, do wait for me.	✗	
g.	Don't forget! You pay for me!	✗	

A. Translate the words in brackets.

Work hard and for many hours, *try* to be honest, and you'll be the darling of the Inland Revenue Office.

B. Which of the following sentences is best?

1. Decide what your level of English is and tick the box.
2. Don't send off the letter until you've signed it.

C. Best word for the gap!

Graffiti: *Make* love not war! (Level I: 8)
Save energy. *Make* love more slowly! (Level I: 8)

D. Translate the German in the brackets.

1. Doctor: *Do that, please.* (Level I: 1)
2. *Don't tell* your friends about your indigestion. (Level I: 3, 8)

E. Complete the imperative.

1. *Don't* tell lies when you can use statistics. (Level I: 6)
2. Sign in a German bar for British soldiers: *Don't* worry how bad our English is. Our Scotch is excellent. (Level I: 6)

F. Time for a *woggle*.

1. She: *Don't* you try, or I'll slap your face. (Level II: 12)
2. Ron: Tell me why people take an instant dislike to me, *will* you! (Level II: 10)
3. Husband to wife: If it's a boy let's call him John, *shall* we? If it's a girl, we could call her Jane, couldn't we? And if it's twins, *let's* call it a day. (Level II: 11)

G. Complete the following.

1. OK, everyone. There's plenty to eat and drink, so *do help yourselves*!
2. I'm tired of staying indoors. I need some fresh air. *Let's go for a walk.* (Level II: 11)
3. I'll be in bed when you come home, so *don't you forget your key.* (Level II: 12)
4. It sounds terribly exciting! *Do tell me about it*! (Level II: 9)
5. Examination in progress. *Do not disturb*! (Level I: 6, 7)
6. *Turn off the electricity supply* before repairing the machine. (Level I: 2)
7. I'm busy, so if anyone phones, *please (do) say I'm out.* (Level I: 1)
8. I'm fed up with going to discos. *Let's go somewhere else* for a change, *shall we*? (Level II: 11)

2. Einfache Zeiten und ihre Verlaufsform
Simple and Progressive Tenses

2

Spot the mistake

a. This cheese ~~is smelling~~ *smells* awful.
b. He *has* ~~waited~~ *been waiting* all day long.
c. It ~~gets~~ *is getting* colder and colder here.
d. Don't wake him up. He ~~sleeps~~ *is sleeping*.

Tick them off

	Right	Wrong
a. Listen! ~~Are you hearing~~ *Do* you *hear* that noise?		✗
b. I'm seeing my doctor tomorrow.	✗	
c. Beer or wine? What ~~are you meaning~~ *do you think*?		✗
d. Sorry, but ~~I'm not understanding~~ *I don't understand* you.		✗
e. I'm having a shower now.	✗	
f. I ~~'m not having~~ *don't have* a car at the moment.		✗
g. The tree has been standing there for 50 years.	✗	

A. Do you know the forms when you see them?

1. *"uses"* ist einfache Zeit (Level I: 1), es ist eine wiederholte Handlung.
2. *"I'm not acting"* ist Verlaufsform (Level I: 2) für eine nicht abgeschlossene Handlung, die zum Zeitpunkt des Sprechens abläuft.

B. Put in the correct form of the verb.

Tim is *explaining* (Level I: 2) the latest copier model to Anita:

Anita: How *do you work* (Level I: 1) this photocopier? I think *I'm doing* (Level I: 2) something wrong.

Tim: Yes, you *are pressing* (Level I: 2) the wrong button. That one *enlarges* (Level I: 1) the copies. You need to press this one.

Anita: Oh yes. It *is working* (Level I: 2) properly now.

C. Which is correct?

1. Guest: Waiter, what is this fly *doing* (Level I: 2) in my soup?
   Waiter: Breasttroke, I suppose.
2. I sold the memoirs of my sex life to a publisher this morning. They are
   making (Level I: 2) a board game out of it. (WOODY ALLEN)

2

D. Is it live or living?

1. San Francisco is the only place where a working-class man *lives* like a
   queen. (Level I: 1)
2. I'*m living* so far beyond my income that we may almost be said to *be li-ving* apart. (Level I: 2)
3. The interior decorator installed a skylight in my apartment. The people
   who *live* above me are furious! (Level I: 1)
4. "I really don't want a lot of money," said Tina. "I just wish we could af-ford to live the way we'*re living* now." (Level I: 2)

E. Choose the right one.

1. An expert is one who *knows* (Level II: 4d) more and more about less
   and less.
2. An optimist *believes* (Level II: 4d) that what's going on will be postponed.
3. Young man: *Do you think* (Level II: 4d) you could be happy with a
   man like me?
   Young woman: Of course! As long as he wasn't too much like you.

F. Match the rules to the example sentences.

1 + D   2 + A   3 + B   4 + C

G. Translate the German in the brackets.

1. Ortrud: *I think* (Level II: 4d) I'd like to be cremated.
   Manfred: Okay love – get your coat on.
2. Bob: *Do you believe* (Level II: 4d) in ghosts?
   René: I don't, but I know they are there, and I *guess / suppose*
   they don't believe in me either.
3. What *do you get* (Level I: 1) if you *cross* (Level I: 1) a terrier with a fire?

H. Progressive or Simple?

A: Good morning. Is Mr. Kleinstück in?

B: Yes, he is, but he *is seeing* (Level II: 5) someone at the moment. *Is he expecting* you? (Level I: 2, *expect* = erwarten, dynamische Bedeutung, siehe unten)

A: Yes, I *have* (Level II: 4) an appointment with him at 10:30. My name's Bossybitch.

B: Ah yes, Mr Bossybitch. I'm afraid we *are running* (Level I: 2) a little late this morning, but I *don't expect* (= *think*, statische Bedeutung; Level II: 4d) Mr Kleinstück will be long, if you *don't mind* (Level II: 4c) waiting.

2

Schlüssel zu den Übungen

3. Über die Gegenwart sprechen – Talking about the Present

Spot the mistake

a. "~~I dance~~ *I'm dancing* a tango, and you?"
b. A professor is someone who ~~is talking~~ *talks* in someone else's sleep.
c. What we ~~are calling~~ *call* work, the Mexicans call siesta.
d. A vegetarian is someone who eats vegetables not because he loves animals, but because he ~~is hating~~ *hates* plants.
e. If it ~~is stinking~~ *stinks*, it's chemistry. If it doesn't work, it's physics.

Tick them off

Right Wrong

a. Whenever I get home from the office my wife is usually watching TV.
b. Your problem is that you're always wishing for something you don't have.
c. Why on earth ~~do you always park~~ *are you always parking* your car in front of our gate?
d. Inflation is when wallets are getting bigger and shopping bags smaller.
e. A wise man ~~is never laughing~~ *never laughs* at his wife's old clothes.
f. The Neckar ~~is flowing~~ *flows* into the river Rhine.

A. Choose the correct Aspect.

The plane *is circling* (Level I: 5) at ten thousand feet, the newly recruited Friesian parachutes *are getting* (Level I: 5) ready for their first jump. "Stop!" shouts the officer. "You *are not wearing* (Level I: 5) your parachute." – "It's okay, captain," replies one of them. "Sure, it's only a practice jump we *are doing* (Level I: 5)."

B. Select the correct Aspect.

1. My wife never *tells* ~~is telling~~ me how to wash the dishes. (Level I: 1, 4)
2. Money *doesn't always bring* ~~isn't always bringing~~ happiness. (Level I: 1, 4)

Key to the Exercises

C. Translate into German.

1. Women's faults are many. Men *have* (Level I: 1,2) only two. Everything they *say* (Level I: 3, 4) and everything they *do* (Level I: 3, 4).
2. "Please keep quiet, Robert! Your father *is trying* (Level I: 5) to read."

D. Put the verbs in the box into the sentences.

1. A study of economics usually *reveals* that the best time to buy anything is last year. (Level I: 4)
2. Teacher: Today we *are trying* to do without our calculators. (Level I: 5)
3. *Are* you *looking* for work, young man? (Level I: 5)
4. *Do* you *want* any help with your maths home work? (Level I: 1)

E. Put the verbs in the brackets in the correct Tense.

A blonde *is tired* (Level II: 6) of hearing blond jokes and *decides* (Level II: 6) to prove people wrong. She *spends* (Level II: 6) weeks studying a map of the United States, and *memorises* (Level II: 6) all the capitals for all the states.

F. Find the English.

"I don't think Dad *knows / understands* (Level I: 1) much about children."
"Why do you say that?" – "Because he's *always sending* (Level II: 8) me to bed when I'm wide awake and *waking* (Level II: 8) me up when I'm sleepy."

G. Spot the mistakes.

Fehler 1:   the vicar is getting up
Richtig: the vicar *gets* up
Erklärung: Level II: 7

Fehler 2:   and is hugging Kathy
Richtig: and *hugs* Kathy (Level II: 7)
Erklärung: wie oben

Fehler 3:   He then is getting up
Richtig: He then *gets* up
Erklärung: wie oben

Fehler 4:   Kathy is needing
Richtig: Kathy *needs* (Level I: 1, 4)
Erklärung: gewohnheitsmäßige Wiederholung, statisches Verb

H. Put in the correct Tenses.

1. Bob *always drinks* a drop of champagne before his evening meal. (Level I: 4)
2. Ron *always goes* jogging before breakfast. (Level I: 4; see also Level II :8)
3. Bob *frequently tells* Ron to stop wasting his time and energy. (Level I: 4)
4. You're *always giving me* your good advice, but you don't do anything yourself. (Level II: 8)
5. You are *constantly moaning* about your body. (Level II: 8)

4. Über die Vergangenheit reden – Talking about the past

Spot the mistake

a. Ron *used to weigh* 95 kilos.
b. I ~~have~~ *visited* Ron in Battle during my autumn holidays.
c. When I arrived at his cottage, Ron ~~worked~~ *was working* in the garden.
d. Anne didn't know that I was coming, but she ~~was cooking~~ *cooked* me a fine meal when I arrived.
e. And every night Ron ~~was making~~ *made* a fire in the open fireplace.
f. Anne got a bottle of wine, Ron got the glasses and I ~~was opening~~ *opened* the bottle.

Tick them off

Right   Wrong

a. Where ~~have you met~~ *did you meet* Ron? — Wrong: ✗
b. I met him in Hollerberg. — Right: ✗
c. He ~~was shooting~~ *shot* at the robber. He was dead immediately. — Wrong: ✗
d. Ron ~~was inviting~~ *invited* me to his cottage the other day. — Wrong: ✗
e. I used to be a werewolf, but I'm all right nooooooooow! — Right: ✗

A. Put in the correct Tense.

1. My mother *had* a terrible accident the other day. (Level I: 1)
   She *had* the right of way, but the other guy had the truck. (Level I: 1)
2. "Sorry I'm late, sir. I *sprained* my ankle when I *was coming* downstairs."
   – "Huh! Another lame excuse." (Level I: 5)
3. No woman has ever shot her husband while he *was doing* the dishes. (Level I: 5)

Schlüssel zu den Übungen

B. Translate the German in the brackets.

1. Bob: What *happened* to that shockproof, waterproof, unbreakable, anti-magnetic watch I *bought* you for your last birthday? (Level I: 1)
   Ron: I lost it.
2. Eric: My father was very disappointed when I *was born.*
   Ernie: Why? *Did* he *want* a girl? (Level I: 2)
   Eric: No, he *wanted* a divorce. (Level I: 2)
3. A car *was driving* (Level I : 5) at 150 miles per hour on the motorway when it was stopped by the police. "Sorry, officer, was I driving too fast?" "No, sir. But you *were flying* (Level I: 5) too low."

C. Find the correct form.

1. A small boy *was standing* (Level I: 5) next to an escalator. He *was looking* (Level I: 5, 6, Level II: 11) at the handrail.
   "No, I was *just waiting* for my chewing gum to come back."
   (Level I: 5, 6, Level II: 11)
2. God was a woman until she *changed* her mind. (Level I: 2)
3. Ron: How *did you get* the splinter in your finger (Level I: 2)
   Bob: All I *did* was scratch my head. (Level I: 2)

D. Find the English for the German in the brackets.

1. Have you noticed that all the things you *used to do* when you were a kid are now being done by batteries. (Level II: 8)
2. What a mean person! She was always heating the knives so that we would use less butter. (Level II: 12)
3. In London a landlady explains to an American guest full of pride: Shakespeare *used to sleep* in this bed. "Well," says the American, you could at least have changed the sheets." (Level II: 8)

E. Build the questions.

1. When *did you start* eating spicy food? (Level II: 7, Level I, 1)
   I started eating spicy food when I was fifteen.
2. When *did you go* on your first date? (Level II: 7, Level I, 1)
   I went on my first date when I was eighteen.
3. Where *did they have* this silly idea? (Level II: 7, Level I, 1)
   They had this silly idea at a pub in Heidelberg.

F. Find the mistakes.

1. Fred was asked how he got his black eye:
   "I *was teaching* my girlfriend the tango, we *were dancing* close together. Then her father came in. How was I to know he was stone deaf?"
   (Level II: 10)
2. I did a lot of running, but I was always getting injured so I *gave* it up. (Level I: 3)
3. An Englishman and an American were shipwrecked on an island. The natives were very friendly and after six months the American was running a light railway, while the Englishman *was still waiting* to be introduced. (Level II: 11)

5. Das englische Perfekt – The Present Perfect

Spot the mistake

a. An intellectual is a man who ~~found~~ *has found* something more interesting than woman

b. I ~~live~~ *have lived* in Bonn for 20 years.

c. Paul and Pauline have known each other ~~since~~ *for* three years.

d. When ~~have started~~ *did you start* to study?

e. I'~~ve met~~ *met* Peter at the station.

f. Bob ~~has been failing~~ *has failed* his exam at least three times.

g. We ~~ve been~~ *were* in Rome on our 25th wedding anniversary.

Tick them off

	Right	Wrong
a. "Thank God! He ~~has been passing~~ *has passed* his exam."		✗
b. "What a mess!" – "Well, *I've been painting* the garage."	✗	
c. I ~~repaired~~ *have repaired* the car. You can continue your trip.		✗
d. I ~~live~~ *have been living* with my mother since Easter because my house burnt down a month ago.		✗
e. We *have known* each other since school.	✗	
f. He *has already* ~~been having~~ *had* three accidents.		✗
g. I ~~am waiting~~ *have been waiting* for you for three hours.		✗

A. Identification game.

1. Level I: 2
2. Level I: 2
3. Level I: 1

B. Find the English for the words in brackets.

1. What do you call a man who *has lost* half of his brain?
   A widower. (Level I: 3)
2. "Darling, do you have a good memory for faces?" – "Yes, I think so.
   Why do you ask?" – "Because I *have* just *broken* your shaving mirror."
   (Level I: 2)
3. No one *has ever complained* of a parachute not opening. (Level I: 2)

C. Which is best? Simple or Progressive?

1. My wife *has been missing* ~~has been missed~~ for two days. I don't know
   whether she has left me or gone shopping. (Level I: 4)
2. After the baptism the vicar praises the parents: "I've never seen such a
   well-behaved baby." – "No wonder," says the proud father. "*We've been
   practising* ~~we have practised~~ all week with a watering can." (Level I: 4, 5)
3. A man bought a parrot at an auction after some very brisk bidding. "I
   hope this bird talks," he said to the auctioneer. "Does he talk? Who do
   you think *has been bidding* ~~has bidded~~ against you for the past twenty
   minutes? (Level I: 4, 5)
4. She *has taken* ~~has been taking~~ fifty of these this anti-fat pills. Now she's
   so thin that every time she walks in the park, a dog tries to bury her.
   (Level I: 3)

D. Spot the mistake.

1. "Mummy, you know that old vase in the hall? The one they*'ve handed*
   down from generation to generation?" (Level I: 1) Well, this generation
   has come to apologise for dropping it." (Level II: 10)
2. "How long *has* old Pedro *been fishing*?" – "I'm not sure, but he's the
   only member of the angling club fishing with a Louis XV rod."
   (Level I: 4, 5)
3. Teaching *has ruined* more American novelists than drink. (Level I: 3)

E. Which is correct?

1. I *have drunk* seven pints of beer since lunchtime and now I'm as drunk as a lord. (Level II: 8)
2. "Hey Jim, *did you see* Sue at the railway station? (Simple Past, Level I: 2) Her train was due at 7 p.m." (Level II: 11)
3. I can't understand the fuss over computer pornography. Surely everybody *has seen* a computer without clothes on by now. (Level I: 3)

F. How would you translate the German in the brackets?

1. The following advertisement *appeared* (Simple Past) in a Scottish newspaper: A gentlemen who *has lost* (Level I: 3) a left leg would like to correspond with another who *has lost* (Level I: 3) his right leg and takes a size nine shoe.
2. "Prisoner, this court *has accused* (Level I: 3, Level II: 10) you of stealing £5,000, but it has been unable to prove you guilty. Therefore, you are now free to go. Do you have anything to say?" – "*Does that mean* (Simple Present) that I can keep the money?"

5

6. Imperfekt und Perfekt im Vergleich
Past and Present Perfect Compared

6

Spot the mistake

a. Why has Australia got all the Kangaroos and Austria all the Austrians? –
   God ~~has given~~ *gave* the Australians the first choice.
b. After man came woman. And she ~~was~~ *has been* after him ever since.
c. Ron: I thought you ~~are~~ *were* on a diet. (Past Tense, denn jetzt denkt er
   es nicht mehr)
d. Baker: I ~~have been making~~ *was making* bread before you were born.
   Customer: Maybe so, but why are you selling it now?

Tick them off

Right Wrong

a. The Pentagon once ~~has paid~~ *paid* $435 for a hammer
   available for $7 in the shops.
b. I ~~already received~~ *have already received* ten
   compliments today.
c. In 1703 the Irish invented the toilet seat.
   In 1704 the English put a hole in it.
d. ~~I've met~~ *I met* a Japanese gentleman who was
   so wealthy that he wanted to buy what he called 'a
   place down South'. It was Australia.

A. Make your choice: Past Tense or Present Perfect.

1. Tramp: I *haven't eaten* ~~didn't eat~~ for three days, mister. (Level I: 4)
2. Anne: ~~Did I ever send~~ *Have I ever sent* you a bill? (Level I: 2)
3. Professionals ~~have built~~ *built* the Titanic. (Level I: 1)
   Amateurs ~~have built~~ *built* the Ark. (Level I: 1)

B. Put the verbs in the brackets into the correct form.

1. Psychiatrist: Nonsense, you worm, you *haven't met* everybody yet.
   (Level I: 3)
2. Bobby: *Have you read* the new Brockhaus Encyclopedia? (Level I: 1)
3. "Hey, barman, I *ordered* a pint." (Level I: 1)

C. Two mistakes in each example for you to correct.

1. Have you been to Egypt? I ~~was~~ *have been* there twice, but there were some things I ~~haven't liked~~ *didn't like*. (Level I: 2), (Level I: 1)
2. "How long ~~have you stayed~~ *did you stay* in Cairo?" I~~'ve been~~ *was* there for three years. Then I went on to Tunisia. (Level I: 4), (Level I: 4)
3. I ~~always wanted~~ *have always wanted* to visit the pyramids. Now I ~~found~~ *have found* I can't stand the climate. (Level I: 2)

D. Present Perfect or Simple Past?

1. Robert: I ~~have visited~~ *visited* the Shetland Islands recently. (Level II: 7)
   Farmer: They drowned when we *tried* ~~have tried~~ to train them for surf riding. (Level I: 1)
2. Policeman: ~~Have you known~~ *Did you know* that your wife fell out of the car two or three kilometres ago? (Level I: 1)
3. I ~~have seen~~ *saw* Bob at the railway station. He was with a pretty blond girl. (Level I: 3)

E. Translate the German in the brackets.

1. Art critics are like eunuchs in a harem; they know how it's done, they *have seen* it done every day. (Level I: 2)
2. Since then we *have taken* a great step forward. (Level II: 5)
3. *Did you hear* about the Scot who won a holiday for two in Majorca? He *went* by himself twice. (Level II: 6), (Level I: 1)

F. Put the words in brackets into the correct form.

1. "I never *lied* when I was a child."
   "So when *did you start*, Sir?" (Level I: 1)
2. "I'm sorry. I *didn't know* it was their turn." (Level I: 1)

7. Die Vorvergangenheit – The Past Perfect

Spot the mistake

a. Just think, if Shakespeare ~~had~~ *had had* a computer, he probably would have accidentally erased *A Midsummer Night's Dream*.

b. Last night I dreamt I had invented a new type of breakfast food. When I woke up in the morning, I found that a corner of the mattress ~~disappeared~~ *had disappeared*.

c. When she asked him why he ~~has~~ *had* suddenly *stopped* loving her, he said he had a train to catch.

Tick them off

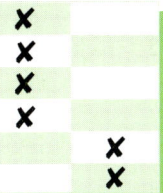

	Right	Wrong
a. When we arrived, she made tea.	✗	
b. When we arrived, she was already making tea.	✗	
c. When we arrived, she had already made tea.	✗	
d. When we had arrived, she made tea.	✗	
e. When we had arrived, she was making tea.		✗
f. When we had arrived, she had made tea.		✗

A. Which form is correct?

1. An applicant who *had just completed* ~~just completed~~ (Level I: 1) a series of multiple choice tests was asked by the teacher whether it pays to be honest. He immediately asked what the five alternatives were.

2. Judge: Now tell me, why did you steal that wallet?
   Prisoner: Your Honour, I ~~hadn't felt~~ *hadn't been feeling well* (Level I: 3) on that day and I thought the change would do me good.

3. A happy event in church:
   After the priest ~~read~~ *had read* (Level I: 2) the fourth commandment: "Thou Shalt Not Steal", I noticed my umbrella was gone. After he ~~read~~ *had read* the seventh commandment: "Thou Shalt Not Commit Adultery"; I suddenly *remembered* ~~had remembered~~ (Simple Past) where I had left it.

B. Put the words in brackets into the right form.

1. "I could always tell when my girlfriend *had been drinking* (Level I: 3). Her face would start getting blurred."
2. Bob: Last night I dreamed that I *had been making love* (Level I: 3) to the most beautiful girl in the world.
   Usch: And how *was* I? (Simple Past)
3. "Doctor, Doctor, I've lost my memory."
   "When *did this happen*?" (Simple Past, abgeschlossene Handlung)
   "When *did* what *happen*?"

C. Merlin's everyday problems.

Merlin *had just come* (Level I: 1) home from work when he *found* (Level I: Simple Past, abgeschlossene Handlung) a leak in his bathroom. Water *had been dripping* (Level I: 3) from the ceiling for some time, and there *was* (Simple Past, abgeschlossene Handlung) a large pool of water on the floor. As soon as he *saw / had seen* (Level II: 6) the leak, he *called* (Simple Past, abgeschlossene Handlung, Handlungskette) the plumber.

The plumber's wife *answered* (Simple Past, abgeschlossene Handlung): "I'm afraid he *went* (Simple Past, abgeschlossene Handlung mit Zeitangabe) out an hour ago and he *hasn't come* (Present Perfect, Schlüsselwort "yet") back yet."

Merlin *had not expected* (Level I: 1) an answer like that. "I'll have to get some magic together and do it that way," he moaned.

D. Create one sentence for each of the following pairs.

1. After / as soon as / when the plane had landed, I took my safety belt off. (Level II: 6)
2. After / as soon as I had left the plane, I noticed my luggage was missing. (Level II: 6)
3. (Of course) I found my luggage lying on the floor after I had complained to the clerk. (Level II: 6)

E. Past Perfect or Past Perfect Progressive?

1. They ~~had driven~~ *had been driving* (Level II: 5) for more than three hours when the trouble in the engine started.
2. Jenny ~~had gone~~ *had been going* (Level II: 5) out with Bill for ten years before she heard about his double life.
3. As soon as I *had read* ~~had been reading~~ (Level I: 1) the e-mail, I phoned the police.
4. Annette *had fallen* ~~had been falling~~ (Level II: 5) asleep at least five times by the time the phone finally rang.

F. Merlin and the modern world (continued).

"I'll give them one more chance," thought Merlin. He *had decided* (Level II: 6) that after an hour or two's thought, because doing magic costs energy and he didn't have too much energy left after he *had spent* (Level I: 1) two days in that police cell. So he sat down to wait for the call. Two hours later the phone *rang* (Simple Past). "This is the plumber. You *called* (Simple Past, mit Zeitangabe "earlier") earlier." – "Where on earth *have* you *been*?" (Present Perfect) demanded the wizard angrily. "I *have been waiting* (Present Perfect mit "for") for two hours! What have you been doing all this time?" – "I'm terribly sorry, sir. No sooner *had* I *left* (Level I: 1) my house to come to you, than I had an accident. After the police *had been questioning* (Level II: 5) me for more than an hour, they realised I wasn't drunk and let me go. That's why I'm late."

8. Über die Zukunft sprechen – Talking about the Future

8

Which is the best choice

a. 2 If the weather is fine tomorrow, *I will* go for a jog.
b. 1 When we get home the kids *will be sleeping*.
c. 2 When we get home *I'll go* to bed immediately.
d. 2 I'm going to visit my mother as soon as *I arrive* in Berlin.
e. 1 When you read this picture postcard *I'll be lying* on the beach in Florida.
f. 1 Let me post this letter for you. On my way home *I'll be passing* the post office anyway.

Tick them off

Right   Wrong

a. Will you still be sending me Valentines when I'm sixty-four?
b. As soon as the German tourist ~~will get~~ *gets* to Paradise, he will ask for picture postcards.
c. Wait for me, I'll have finished this letter in a couple of minutes.
d. Tomorrow's cars ~~are looking~~ (*will*) *look* quite different.

A. Which of our Level I rules fits which sentence?

1. Level I: 1d   **2.** Level I: 2 b   **3.** Level I: 4

B. Which Future fits best?

1. b. Eat, drink and be happy – for tomorrow we *(will) diet*. (Level I: 1a)
2. a. Ron: I *am going to go* now. (Level I: 2a)
3. b. You'll *be* old and weak yourself one day, too. (Level I: 1a)

C. Put in the most appropriate Future form.

1. "Doctor, I'm afraid *I'm going to die.*"(Level I: 2b)
   "Nonsense, that's the last thing you'll do."
2. Fat Bessie Braddock to Winston Churchill:
   "Winston, you are drunk."
   "Bessie, you are ugly. But tomorrow *I'll be* sober." (Level I: 1a)
3. He: Darling, if we get married do you think you *will be able* to live on my income? (Level I: 1a, b)
   She: Of course, darling, but what *are you going to live on*? (Level I: 2a)

D. What do the following sentences express?

1. c. Bitte um Voraussage (Level I: 1a)
2. c. Absicht, Vorhaben (Level I: 2)
3. a. Teil einer bereits geplanten Situation (Level II: 5)

E. Choose the most appropriate form of the Future.

1. a. Tycoon: Well then, how many shares *are you going to buy*.
   (Level I: 2a)
2. a. René: Yes, *I'll be playing* chess with my dog. (Level II: 5, 6)
3. c. Tailor: Your suit *will be* ready in six month, sir. (Level I: 1 a, c)

8

9. Indirekte Rede – Indirect Speech

Spot the mistake

a. Tina thought Robinson Crusoe ~~is~~ *was* a world famous tenor.
b. The first time the little girl from the big city ever saw a cow she thought it was a bull that ~~has~~ *had* swallowed a glove.
c. Have you heard about the Irish explorer who paid £10 for a sheet of sandpaper? – He thought ~~it's~~ *it was* a map of the Sahara Desert.
d. An Irish professor announced that he ~~has~~ *had* performed his first appendix transplant.

Tick them off

	Right	Wrong
a. "An alcoholic," my doctor told me, "is a person who drinks more than his doctor."	✗	
b. I told my psychiatrist that I didn't believe in reincarnation last time, either.	✗	
c. Tim told his teacher he was so poor, he ~~can't~~ *couldn't* even pay attention.		✗
d. He whispered into my ear that the new accountant ~~has~~ *had* all the characteristics of a dog – except loyalty.		✗
e. Sometimes I think that God, in creating man, somewhat overestimated his ability. (OSCAR WILDE)	✗	

A. What did they actually say?

1. Anne: Henrietta, I will be glad when we have eaten the last of the rhinoceros. (Level I: 3g)
2. Jim: Nothing that is worth knowing can be taught. (Level I: 3b)
3. Bob: My petrol tank has sprung a leak. (Level I: 3e)

B. Make your choice.

1. "I'm informed from many quarters that a rumour ~~had~~ *has* been put about that I died this morning. This is quite untrue." (Level I: 2)
2. And there was the Irish helicopter pilot who thought it *was* too cold. (Level I: 3 a)

3. Eve was the most frustrated of women: she couldn't nag Adam by telling him what a wonderful man her first husband ~~is~~ *was*. (Level I: 3a)

C. Put the following into Indirect Speech.

1. Bob said a genius *was* anybody who could describe how an accordion *worked* without using his hands. (Level I: 3a)
2. Ron asked which book Anne *liked* best. Anne replied she *liked* her husband's chequebook most. (Level I: 3a)
3. G. B. Shaw commented that old age *was* not so bad when you *considered* the alternative. (Level I: 3a)
   Ron said he *would be driving* to Spain in summer. (Level I: 3g)

D. Translate the verbs in brackets into the correct form.

1. When a Texas school class was told that next day they *would learn* to draw, eighteen boys turned up with pistols. (Level II: 5b)
2. Bob told Ron that he *could not believe* a word he was saying, so he certainly couldn't believe any of Ron's sentences. (Level II: 5b)
3. Ron's old stories about himself: he was telling us that he only *needed* four minutes to run a mile. (Level II: 5a)

E. Spot the mistake.

1. Ron said that he ~~doesn't need~~ *didn't need* to answer the question. (Level II: 3a)
2. Sue said she ~~may be~~ *might be* late. (Level II: 5b)
3. Salesman: Sir, my wife said I ~~shall ask~~ *should ask* for a raise. (Level II: 5b)
   Sales Manager: I'll ask my wife if I may give ~~might give~~ you one. (Level II: 5b)

F. Put the sentences into Indirect Speech.

1. He suggested having a short holiday. (Level II: 6)
2. He offered her the use of his car. (Level II: 6)
3. He absolutely refused to accept it. (Level II: 6)
4. He warned her to watch what she was doing! (Level II: 6b)

9

Schlüssel zu den Übungen

10. Indirekte Fragen und Anweisungen – Indirect Questions and Instructions

10

Spot the mistake

a. If someone asks me, what ~~is~~ two and two *is*, I answer "Are you buying or selling?"
b. He asked her *to* bring ~~me~~ *him* the book.
c. The electrician complained that people asked him ~~come~~ *to come* and repair the bell and then didn't open the door.

Tick them off   Right   Wrong

a. "I'd like to know how long ~~can~~ a human being *can* live without a brain." – "Well, how old are you?"   ✗
b. Do you know what ~~is~~ the difference *is* between a chess player and a civil servant? ... Well, a chess player moves every now and then.   ✗
c. He asked me if I knew ~~who~~ *where* the new supermarket ~~is~~ *was*?   ✗

A. What did they actually say?

1. Teacher: Today we are trying to do without our calculators. What is 3 x 7?
   Pupil: When are we to hand in the results? (Level I: 1 – 4)
2. He: Why is George a born executive?
   She: Because his father owns the business. (Level I: 1 – 4)
3. Ron: How do you double the price of a Trabi?
   Bob: Fill up the petrol tank. (Level I: 1 – 4)

B. Report what they said.

1. Bob commented that he didn't like tongue in wine sauce. He went on that the idea of eating something that had been in a cow's mouth disgusted him (see chapter: Indirekte Rede, Aussagen). Ron asked him if he ate eggs. (Level I: 2)

2. Bob wanted to know if Alcoholics Anonymous wasn't a place where whisky was drunk in secret. (Level I: 2)
3. The sign in the undertaker's window told people to drive carefully because they could wait. (Level I: 5)

C. Convert the following sentences into Indirect Speech.

1. He advised her to check it out before she spent the money. (Level I: 6)
2. He invited her to join him on his trip to Egypt. (Level I: 7)
3. He warned her to be careful what she said to Helen because she was very sensitive. (Level I: 6)
4. The boss told the secretary that if Mr. Walker called before he returned, she should tell him to call again at 5 o'clock. (see chapter: Indirekte Rede, Aussagen). However, she wanted to know what to tell him if didn't call. (Level I: 4)

D. Put the following sentences into Indirect Speech.

1. A worried young girl told her doctor that the new diet he had put her on made her feel so passionate and sexy that she had got carried away the night before and had bitten off her boyfriend's ear. The doctor advised her not to worry because it was only forty to fifty calories. (Level II: 9 – 12)
2. During the war two German spies were in a pub in London. They didn't want to be recognised as Germans so one of them ordered in English and asked for two martinis. The barman asked if they should be dry, to which the German replied that he wanted "zwei" not "drei" martinis. (Level II: 9 – 12)
3. The slogan on a mechanic's T-shirt said that he shouldn't be asked anything as he was only hired for his looks. (Level II: 9 – 12)

E. What did they really say.

1. Bob: Do you want to go walking with me in the Black Forest? (Level II: Sprachfallen)
2. Ron: This German system is shocking and unbelievable. (Level II: Sprachfallen)
3. She: My God, I've dropped the plate. (Level II: Sprachfallen)

10

F. Spot the mistake.

1. An elderly lady entered a pet shop and said to the shop assistant that she ~~is~~ *was* disappointed with the canary she had been sold. She complained that it ~~is~~ *was* lame (see chapter Indirekte Rede, Level I: 3a). The shop assistant asked her whether she ~~wants~~ *wanted* (Level II: 9) a singer or a dancer.

2. Shortsighted old Bob browsing in the antique shop: He asked the shop assistant what that old figure ~~is~~ *was* (Level II: 9a) worth and she replied it ~~is~~ *was* (see chapter Indirekte Rede, Level I: 3a) worth about £200,000, but ~~that's it's~~ that *it was* (see chapter Indirekte Rede, Level I: 3a) the owner.

10

11. Aktiv und Passiv – Active and Passive Voice

Spot the mistake

a. This money was promised to me ~~from~~ *by* Dr Bossy.
b. The poor chap was killed ~~by~~ *with* a knife.
c. Turn on the radio. An interesting programme is *being* broadcast at the moment.
d. ~~About~~ This scandal was spoken *about* again and again.
e. Grandma Mary enjoys ~~to be told~~ *being told* about our plans.

Tick them off

	Right	Wrong
a. An egg is something that is never beaten when it is bad.	✗	
b. Tom is considered *to be* the best salesman. He can sell refrigerators to Eskimos.		✗
c. Abstinence is a good thing, but it should be practised in moderation.	✗	
d. I'm living so far beyond my income that we may almost be said to be living apart.	✗	
e. I don't believe you. This photo ~~can't be~~ *can't have been* taken in Japan.		✗

A. Identify the Passives.

1. to be examined / to be admired = Infinitive Passive (Level I: Infinitive)
2. he is hired = Simple Present (Level I: Simple Present)
3. Kein Passiv, sondern Aktiv

B. Convert Active into Passive and vice versa.

1. Jenny, you *are wanted* on the phone. (Level I: Simple Present)
2. Our books *are sold* more cheaply in Russia. (Level I: Simple Present)
3. Let's hope they *can be persuaded* not to cancel the order. (Level I: Modal)
4. They *will be offered* special conditions. (Level I: Future)

5. If you see a gun fight, get into it, so they *won't shoot* you as a bystander. (Level I: Future)
6. A woman *wears* high heels when she no longer wants to be kissed on her forehead. (Level I: Simple Present)

C. Build Passive sentences.

1. Government corruption is always reported in the past tense. (Level I: Simple Present)
2. If they didn't, *they would be married, too.* (Level I: Modal)
3. *I've been vaccinated.* (Level I: Present Perfect)

D. Build Passive sentences.

1. If man had to be meant to fly he *would have been born* with wings. (see chapter Konditionalsätze, Typ II)
2. For every person wishing to teach there are thirty persons who *don't want to be taught.* (Level I: Infinitive)
3. She *has been divorced by* fifteen husbands – and she's kept all the fifteen houses. (Level I: Present Perfect)

E. Change into the Passive.

1. Visitors *must be accompanied* by staff members at all times. (Level I: Modals)
2. Handbooks *must not be removed* from the copiers. (Level I: Modals)
3. Mobiles *can be borrowed* on request. (Level I: Modals)

F. Put in the correct Passive forms.

1. Bob: When I was seven years old *I was taken to* London Zoo. (Level I: Past Simple)
   Ron: Were *you accepted*? (Level I: Past Simple)
2. It *is hoped* (Level I: Simple Present), it *will be rebuilt* by the end of the week. (Level I: Future)
3. If paintings can *be forged* (Level I: Modals) well enough to fool experts, why is the original so valuable?

12. Modale Hilfsverben – Modal Auxiliaries

12

Spot the mistake

a. I ~~mustn't~~ *needn't* tell my wife anything. My neighbours do it for me.
b. Tom is a genius. He ~~can~~ *can do* everything. He ~~can~~ *can* even *speak* Chinese.
c. "Doctor! Whenever I try to drink tea my eye hurts. What ~~will~~ *shall* I do?"
   – "Hmmm! Try taking the spoon out of the glass!"

Tick them off

	Right	Wrong
a. An Italian prime minister *ought not to* think of getting married until he gets a steady job.	✗	
b. A pub advertises: Our steaks are so tender that we don't know how that cow ~~might~~ *was able to* walk.		✗
c. "Daddy," said the bright child accompanying her father on a round of golf. "Why *mustn't* the ball go into the little hole?"	✗	
d. It's the final proof of God's omnipotence that he ~~mustn't~~ *needn't* exist in order to save us.		✗

A. Put in the modal which fits best.

1. **b.** I think if I have a good breakfast I *could* go without food for the rest of the day. (Level I: 1a)
2. **d.** "My wife has everything a man *could* want," said the tiny man from Mars (Level I: 1c)
3. **c.** Mother: Ron's teacher says he *ought* to have an encyclopaedia. (Level I: 5b)

B. Translate the German in the brackets.

1. But the bulb *must want* to be changed. (Level I: 4a)
2. God grant that I *may catch* a fish (Level I: 2a) – so big that even I, when speaking of it to my friends, *may not* lie. (Level I: 2a)
3. That *must have been* beginner's luck. (Level I: 4c)

C. What do the following modals really express?

1. c Schlussfolgerung, Gewissheit (Level I: 4c)

2. a Bitte, Wunsch (Level I: 3a)

D. Put in the correct form of the modal.

1. a Archduke Franz Ferdinand having been found alive, the first World War *must have been* a mistake. (Level I: 4c)

2. b Anyone who *has to* see a psychiatrist needs to have his head examined. (Level II: 7)

3. a "And you *will have to* cut out drinking, smoking and sex."(Level I: 6)

E. Find the suitable modal for the German in brackets.

1. My husband is on a diet of coconuts and bananas. He hasn't lost any weight, but you *should see* him climbing trees. (Level II: 8)

2. "I *don't need to* be faster then the lion," replied Bob. "I only *mustn't* be slower than you!" (Level II: 7, Sprachfallen 5)

3. A wise man *must be able* to hire people who are wiser than himself. (Level II: Sprachfallen 4)

F. Make your choice.

1. Bob: Ron, if you've got liver problems you *mustn't* ~~needn't~~ drink any alcohol. (Level II: Sprachfallen 5)

2. Bob: Ron, I heard you ~~can~~ *can speak* Russian. Why don't you try to do business in Russia? (Level II: Sprachfallen 1)

3. "*Would* ~~will~~ you also like the feathers, sir?" (Level II: 9)

13. Konditionalsätze – Conditional Sentences

13

Spot the mistake

a. If I ~~would have~~ *had* to live my life again, I'd start making the same mistakes earlier.
b. My wife says ~~she leaves~~ she'*ll leave* me if I don't throw out my computer. I'll miss her.
c. Nobody is allowed to spit in a man's face unless his beard ~~will be~~ *is* on fire.

Tick them off

Right Wrong

a. If the Germans don't buy our English beef, we won't drink their whisky. **✗** (Right)
b. Bob, at a repair shop: Please change the oil.
   Mechanic: If I ~~would be~~ *were* you, I'd keep the oil and change the car. **✗** (Wrong)
c. If only God ~~gave~~ *would give* me a clear sign! Like making a large deposit in my name at a Swiss bank. **✗** (Right)
d. God ~~had never~~ *would never have given* us the bicycle if he had wanted us to walk. **✗** (Wrong)

A. Do you know a conditional sentence when you see it?

1. F – Fragesatz
2. F – Fragesatz
3. B – Bedingungssatz
4. F – Fragesatz

B. Complete the following conditional sentences.

1. If you *are* over eighty and accompanied by your parents, we will cash your cheque. (Level I: Type I, a, b)
2. Now, what steps *would you take*, if I dropped this bottle. (Level I: Type II, b)
3. We owe a lot to Edison – if it *weren't* (*wasn't*) for him we'd be watching TV by candle light. (Level I: Type II, a,b)
4. If you are unable to decide between two things, do whichever *is* cheapest. (Level I: Type I, b)

C. Make questions to the following answers.

1. What would you do if you won a million pounds? (Level I: Type II, a, b)
2. What would you do if you lost your present job? (Level I: Type II, a, b)
3. What will you do when you get out of hospital? (Level I: Type I, c)

13

D. What's your opinion?

1. No (Level I: Type III)
2. No (Level I: Type II)
3. Yes (Level I: Type I)

E. Find the full form of I'd, we'd etc.

1. Of course it would have been nicer if *they had* waited for the plane to land. (Level I: Type III)
2. God would never have given us the bicycle if *he had* wanted us to walk. (Level I: Type III)
3. If *Moses had* had a committee, the Israelites'd still be in Egypt. (Level II: 12)
4. Our modern world is so full of problems that if Moses came down from Mount Sinai again, the two tablets he *would be* carrying would be aspirins. (Level I: Type II)
5. "*What would* you do if you found a million pounds, Mike?" (Level II: 12) – "*I would* certainly return it." (Level II: 9)

F. Which form is correct?

1. c. If I had been the Virgin Mary, I *would have said* "No". (Level I: Type III)
2. b. "If you *had been born* a few days ago without any clothes (Type III), and owed £ 2000 on the national debt, you would be crying, too (Type II)."

G. Translate the German into English.

1. It is always the best policy to tell the truth, provided that you are an excellent liar. (Level II: 9)
2. Friendship: An emotion so sweet, steady, loyal and enduring that it lasts a lifetime – unless asked to lend money. (Level II: 9)
3. God would never have given us the example, unless he had wanted us to write on walls. (Level II: 9)

13

H. Put in the correct forms of the Conditionals.

1. More husbands would leave home if they *knew* how to pack their suitcases. (Level I: Type II)
2. If you *would all stop* talking, perhaps we could get on with the meeting. (Level II: 10)
3. If God *had been* a Liberal, we wouldn't have the Ten Commandments – we'd have the Ten Suggestions. (Level II: 12)
4. Ron: What would you do in case you *had* rabies? (Level II: 9)
   Bob: I *would ask* for a pencil and a sheet of paper. (Level I: Type II)
   Ron: For your last will and testament?
   Bob: No, to make a list of the people I *would bite*. (Level I: Type II)

14. Frageanhängsel – Question Tags

Spot the mistake

14

a. You are going on holiday, ~~or~~ *aren't you*?
b. I am right, ~~amn't I~~ *aren't I*?
c. Tim often comes too late, ~~doesn't Tim~~ *doesn't he*?
d. There is a sauna in your hotel, ~~isn't it~~ *isn't there*?
e. Tom had an accident, ~~hadn't he~~ *didn't he*? (*had* ist hier Vollverb)
f. He can't have told us the truth, ~~can't he~~ *can he*?
g. He is never on time, ~~isn't he~~ *is he*?

A. Put in the appropriate Question Tag.

1. Doctor: You're troubled with sexual fantasies, *aren't you*? (Level I: 1)
Patient: Oh no, doc. I rather enjoy them.
2. Woman: If I give you a fine lunch, you won't come back again, *will you*? (Level I: 2)
3. The doctor was giving little Jenny a check-up: "Now, young lady, I'm going to take your pulse."
"No, please don't," cried the girl. "I'll need it, *won't I*?" (Level I: 1)

B. Make your choice.

1. c. Our chancellor is not so stupid as he seems; he couldn't be, *could he*? (Level I: 2)
2. b. "Marriage is a lottery, *isn't it*? (Level I: 1)
3. a. "I can't tell until I've heard the evidence, *can I*? (Level I: 2)

C. Spot the mistake.

1. "Mary was a relative of yours, ~~isn't she~~ *wasn't she*?" (Level I: 1)
2. "Your husband's a hard drinker, ~~is he~~ *isn't he*?" (Level I: 1)
3. "It was mad, ~~it was~~ *wasn't it*? (Level I: 1)

D. Find a suitable Question Tag.

1. c. "He should look well, *shouldn't he*?" said his wife. (Level I: 1)
2. c. "Nonsense, man," said the doctor, "you're imagining things, *aren't you*?" (Level I: 1)
3. a. Well, I am a fool, *aren't I*? (Level II: 5)

E. Choose the Question Tag.

1. b. Angry father: *Oh, you do, do you*? (Level II: Sprachfallen)
2. a. Ticket inspector: "Oh, you can't, *can't you*? (Level II: Sprachfallen)
3. a. Policeman: Oh, you haven't, *haven't you*? (Level II: Sprachfallen)

F. There are some Question Tags that are more difficult.

1. Son: Mum, I needn't go to school today, *need I*? All the teachers hate me and so do the children.
2. "You'd better pay attention, *hadn't you*? You're driving on the pavement." "Oh, I thought you were driving."
3. You'd rather go, *wouldn't you*?
4. Please be quiet, *will you*?
5. He never used to be so fat, *did he*?

Schlüssel zu den Übungen

15. Relativsätze – Relative Clauses

Spot the mistake

a. A coward is a man ~~in who~~ *in whom* the instinct of self-preservation acts normally.

b. Culture is anything ~~what~~ *that* we do and ~~what~~ *that* the monkeys don't.

c. A theologian is a blind man in a dark room who is searching for a black cat ~~who~~ *which* is not there – and he finds it.

Tick them off
<table>
<tr><th></th><th>Right</th><th>Wrong</th></tr>
<tr><td>a. A pedestrian is a man who has a car and ~~his~~ whose son is home from college.</td><td></td><td>✗</td></tr>
<tr><td>b. A friend is someone who dislikes the same people as you. (Kein Komma!)</td><td></td><td>✗</td></tr>
<tr><td>c. Planning is the art of putting off until tomorrow ~~which~~ what you have no intention of doing today.</td><td></td><td>✗</td></tr>
<tr><td>d. Life is ~~that~~ what happens while you are making other plans.</td><td></td><td>✗</td></tr>
<tr><td>e. The honeymoon is the period during which the bride trusts the bridegroom's word of honour.</td><td>✗</td><td></td></tr>
</table>

A. Identify which type they are.

1. a. question word

2. b. relative pronoun (Level I: Type I, A, B 1)

3. b. relative pronoun (Level I: Type I, 1 A, B)

B. Put in the correct Pronoun.

1. A baby is an angel *whose* wings decrease as his legs increase. (Level I: Type I, 4.)

2. A husband is someone *who* will share with you all the problems you wouldn't have had in the first place, if you had not married him. (Level I: Type I, A, B 1)

3. Any programme *that / which* depends on human reliability is unreliable. (Level I: Type I, A, B 1)

C. Use a suitable Relative to join the sentences.

1. A pessimist is a man *who* thinks all women are bad. An optimist hopes so. (Level I: Type I, A, B 1)
2. An acquaintance is a person *whom* we know well enough to borrow money from, but not well enough to lend money to. (Level I: Type I, B 2)
3. A tree is an object *which* will stand in one place for years and then suddenly jump in front of a lady driver. (Level I: Type I, A, B 1)

15

D. Use Relative Pronouns instead of dashes.

1. Englishmen hate two things, *which* are racial discrimination and Irishmen. (Level II: Type II, B 2, 5)
2. Do you remember Jack, *who* died with his boots on? One was on the accelerator. (Level II: Type II, A 1)
3. Friendship is like money, *both of which* are easier made than kept. (Level II: Type II, B 3)

E. Make your choice.

1. **b** of what (Level II: Sprachfallen, 3, 5)
2. **b** of which (Level I: Type I, B 3)
   d of which (Level I: Type I, B 3)
   e of whom (Level I: Type I, B 3)

F. Put in the commas where necessary.

1. There are more men than women in mental *hospitals, which* just goes to show who's driving who crazy. (Level II: Type II, 5)
2. Concorde travels at twice the speed of *sound, which is fun*, except that you can't hear the movie until two hours after you land. (Level II: Type II, 5)
3. Farmer Jack's special *chicken, which* lays rectangular eggs, cost him nearly £ 500. (Level II: Type II, B 1)

G. Choose the Relative Pronoun.

1. I've never visited China, ~~what~~ *which* is a thing I've always wanted to do. (Level II: Sprachfallen 1)
2. Her boss really didn't like ~~that what~~ *what* she said to him. (Level II: Sprachfallen 5)
3. If you tell me *what* ~~all what~~ you know, I may let you go free. (Level II: Sprachfallen 3)

16. Der Infinitiv mit und ohne "to" – The Infinitive with and without "to"

16

Spot the mistake

a. An adult is somebody who has stopped ~~to grow~~ *growing* vertically but not horizontally.
b. The formula for failure – try ~~pleasing~~ *to please* everyone.
c. He may drink to forget, but he never forgets ~~drinking~~ *to drink*.
d. Small boy watching his Mum ~~to do~~ *do* the washing. "Mum, where did you work before you got this job here with us?"

Tick them off

	Right	Wrong
a. "Why are you jumping up and down like that?" "Because I've just taken some medicine and I *forgot to shake* the bottle."	✗	
b. Yesterday I went to the doctor about my bad memory. He ~~made me to pay~~ *made me pay* in advance.		✗
c. Have you heard about the Scotsman who took his wife's false teeth to work with him every day to *stop her eating* between meals?	✗	
d. Most of those who would ~~like moving~~ *like to move* mountains don't like practising on the little hills.		✗

A. Make your choice.

1. You can *lead* ~~to lead~~ a horse to water, but you can't *make* ~~to make~~ it drink. (Level I: A 3)
2. Bob was the first man in Barbados *to make* ~~make~~ a million dollars. (Level I: B 1)
3. Please let me *drive* ~~to drive~~ the car. Nobody's looking. (Level I: A 1)

B. Put "to" into the sentences where necessary.

1. Nothing is illegal if a hundred businessmen decide *to* do it. (Level I: B 2)
2. If you want *to* forget all your troubles, wear a pair of tight shoes. (Level I: B 2)
3. I'd rather *have* my peace and quiet than all this stress. (Level I: A 2)

C. Translate the German in the brackets.

1. Some people would *prefer to be* wrong than to keep quiet. (Level I: B 2)
2. You *had better learn* to swim if you're going on a sailing holiday. (Level I: A 2)
3. An optimist is a man who goes into a restaurant, orders oysters, and *expects to* pay the bill with the pearls he'll find inside them. (Level I: B 2)

D. Ing-form or Infinitive?

1. a   The formula for failure – *try to please* everybody. (Level III: 2)
2. a/b *Try* not *to become* a man of success but rather *try becoming* a man of value. (Level III: 2)
3. b   If you think nothing is impossible, try *getting* your name off a mailing list. (Level III: 2)

E. Make your choice.

1. I much prefer ~~to travel~~ *travelling* in non-British ships. There's none of the nonsense about women and children first. (Level II: B 1)
2. Salesman: Anyone who needs *to ask* ~~asking~~ a question like that, sir, can't afford one. (Level I: B 2)
3. Don't forget *to imitate* ~~imitating~~ the behaviour of winners when you lose. (Level III: 4)

F. Spot the mistake.

1. If you want *to know* the value of money, go and try to borrow some. (Level I: B 2, Level II: B 1)
2. Ron: I hate paying my income tax. (*No mistake* Level II: B 1)
3. He: I know and you expect me *to eat* them. (Level I: B 2)

17. Das Gerund, die andere "-ing"-Form – The Gerund, the other "-ing" form

Spot the mistake

a. If at first you don't succeed, try, try again. Then give up. *It's no use* ~~to be~~ *being* a damned fool about it.

b. When in Paris, I always eat at the Eiffel Tower restaurant because it's the only place where I can *avoid* ~~to see~~ *seeing* the damned thing.

c. Most of those who *would like* ~~moving~~ *to move* mountains don't like practising on the little hills.

Tick them off

	Right	Wrong
a. Imagine the whole world *being* created in six days! Fortunately we now have the trade unions.	✗	
b. Can you *imagine* ~~to live~~ *living* in a city entirely under glass? We'd never have to worry about cold or rain or snow again. Just little kids with rocks!		✗
c. I *used to suffer* from a split personality, Doc, but now we're both okay!	✗	
d. I'll never *get used to living* in a big city.	✗	
e. Nothing *worth learning* is learned quickly, except parachuting.	✗	

A. Infinitive or Gerund.

1. Motorist: Would you mind *putting* ~~to put~~ 90 m.p.h. on the form? I'd like to show it to the man I'm selling it to. (Level I: 3a)

2. Assistant: I know. But he insisted on *being* ~~to be~~ wrong. (Level I: 3c)

3. My way ~~to joke~~ *of joking* is to tell the truth. (Level I: 3c)

B. Translate the words in the brackets.

1. I *would like to* buy my girlfriend a ring, but I don't know what she'd like." (I / He / *She would like to* immer Infinitiv mit "to")

2. Time is nature's *way of preventing everything from happening at the same time.* (Level I: 3c)

3. The art of medicine *consists in amusing the patient* while nature cures the disease. (Level I: 3c)

C. Put in the correct form.

1. b. *Smoking* is something you should not do, if you want to be a competitive athlete. (Level I: 2a)
2. a. He's very good *at talking*. That's why he became a salesman. (Level I: 3c)
3. a. That was a pleasant phone-call. I look forward *to seeing* you later. (Level I: 3c)

17

D. Match the meanings against the forms. (Level II: 7)

1. I stopped helping Mary. She was too difficult.
   a. Ich habe aufgehört ihr zu helfen.
2. The policeman went on examining the criminal.
   b. Der Polizist fuhr mit der Überprüfung fort.
3. I propose to leave Germany and live on an island.
   a. Ich habe die Absicht, Deutschland zu verlassen.

E. "Used to" or "am used to -ing"?

1. a. I *used to be* a werewolf, but I'm alright noooooow! (Level II: Sprachfallen)
2. b. Anita was so mean she *used to heat* the knives so the family would use less butter. (Level II: Sprachfallen)
3. a. I *used to be* arrogant. Now I'm perfectly okay. (Level II: Sprachfallen)

F. Spot the mistake.

Bob: Ron, I'm going to run in the Heidelberg Marathon.

Ron: Are you crazy? You'll risk ~~to get~~ *getting* a heart attack. (Level I: 3a)

Bob: Rubbish. You know I enjoy ~~to run~~ *running* in the open air. There's nothing better. (Level I: 3a)

Ron: But you intended ~~doing~~ *to do* (see chapter Infinitive) that competition next year. What changed your mind?

Bob: Ron, it's very easy. I don't want to miss ~~to eat~~ *eating* my fill at the "Pasta Party" the day before. (Level I: 3a)

18. Die Partizipien – The Participles

Spot the mistake

a. Tim was ~~swiming~~ *swimming* in the pool.
b. I watched the blond girl ~~arresting~~ *being arrested* by the detective.
c. Behind every successful man is a woman ~~wanted~~ *wanting* a fur coat.
d. I heard the phone ~~ringing~~ *ring* only once.

Tick them off

Right   Wrong

a. I *watched* the sun *setting* behind the mountain.
b. I *watched* the boats *sail* out of the harbour.
c. They remained ~~seated~~ *sitting and* ~~eated~~ *eating* at the table.
d. Gentlemen, please *remain seated*.
e. The country lay ~~covering~~ *covered* in snow.
f. The dog *lay dying* on the road.

A. Use a Relative Clause instead of the Participle.

1. The detective wanted to have a word with Merlin *who was standing* next to the bar. (Level I: 1a, c)
2. He thought Merlin could help him to find the pictures *that / which had been stolen* from the museum. (Level I: b, c)
3. Merlin led him to a street map *that / which was hanging* on the wall, murmured a few words and with his wand he made a cross on it. (Level I: 1a, c)

B. Identify the Participles.

1. An oyster is a fish *built* ~~building~~ like a nut. (Level I: 1b, c)
2. Tina: I saw him *sunbathing* ~~sunbathed~~ and he looked so different without his wallet. (Level I: 1a, d, 3)
3. A consultant is a man (or woman) ~~calling~~ *called* in to share the blame. (Level I: 1b, c)

C. Replace the Participles. Use a suitable Conjunction.

1. *If* the weather permits, we'll go for a walk. (Level I: 2d)
2. He took no notice of us, *as* he was interested in what was happening at the other side of the street. (Level I: 2e)
3. *While* we were walking through the park, we had a lively discussion. (Level I: 2a)

D. Translate the German in the brackets.

1. I was teaching my girlfriend the tango when her father *came rushing in*. How was I to know he was stone deaf? (Level I: 1, Level II: 4)
2. The Health Minister, visiting a mental hospital, had difficulty getting the telephone connection to London. *Frustrated* (Level I: 1b) he shouted to the operator, "Young lady, do you know who I am?" *Unmoved* (Level I: 1b) the operator replied, "no sir, but I know where you are."

E. Find the meaning of participle sentences from the context.

1. He welcomed us *and* bowed politely to all of us. (Level II: 4)
2. *As soon as* she entered her bedroom she turned on the lights. (Level I: 2, a)
3. He took no notice of us, *as* he was interested in what was happening at the other side of the street. (Level I: 2, e)

F. Put the verbs in the brackets into the correct form.

1. Tom: I can't believe John is in hospital. I've just seen him *hugging* and *kissing* a beautiful young blond girl in a restaurant. (Level II: 3)
2. To get something *done* a committee should consist of no more than three men, two of whom are absent. (Level II: 4)
3. The newly elected member of Parliament, nervously *searching* (Level I: 1a) for the manuscript for his speech, became even more nervous when *asked* (Level I: 1b, Level II, Sprachfallen) by the speaker: "Are you ready or shall we let them enjoy themselves a bit longer?"

G. Make your choice.

1. **b.** The telephone will ring when you are having a shower. You will reach it just in time to hear the click of the caller *hanging* up. (Level II: 3)
2. **c.** Since the introduction of computers at the workplace, I'm now the second smartest thing *sitting* at my desk. (Level I: 1a)
3. **b.** "It's nice of you, doctor, *to send* my wife away for a rest. Heaven knows, I need it."

19. Der bestimmte Artikel – The Definite Article

19

Spot the mistake

a. ~~The university~~ University is an institution for the postponement of experience.
b. Amusement is ~~happiness~~ *the happiness of those* who cannot think.
c. What sort of people go to ~~the~~ Heaven? – Dead ones.
d. ~~The~~ *Most* young blokes stop looking for work the moment they get a job.
e. The most dangerous part of our expedition to Africa was crossing ~~the~~ *Piccadilly Circus.*

Tick them off

	Right	Wrong
a. The art of medicine consists in amusing the patient while ~~the~~ *nature* cures the disease.		✗
b. My wife is *the most* wonderful woman in the world, and that's not just my opinion – it's hers.	✗	
c. *Most women* are not as young as they are painted.	✗	
d. *The dinner last night* was excellent.	✗	
e. ~~The dinner~~ *Dinner* is ready. Come in at once.		✗

A. You decide! With or without "the"?

1. Don't you love *nature* (Level I: 1), despite what it did to you?
2. There are worse things in *life* (Level I: 1) than *death* (Level I: 1). Have you ever spent an evening with an insurance salesman?
3. "I hear you are going into *hospital* (Level II: 7) next week for a brain operation. The doctors hope to give you one."
   "Yes, I believe it's *the hospital* where you got yours." (Level I: Globalregel)

19

B. Translate the German in the brackets.

1. *Love* (Level I: 1) is only a dirty trick played on us by *evolution* (Level I: 1, Globalrgeel) to achieve the continuation of the species.
2. *Death* (Level I: 1) means stopping sinning suddenly.
3. Meetings: All important decisions will be made in the last five minutes *before lunch* or at the end of the day. (Level I: 3)
4. *The politics* we are experiencing at the moment will destroy Europe. (Level I: 1 näher bestimmt)

C. Spot the mistakes.

1. You can always tell when there is a national catastrophe in *the United States* (Level I: 5). *The President* puts black armbands around his golf clubs (Level I: Globalregel).
2. Believe it or not. *Alcohol* makes you fat. (Level I: 2)
3. In *the* Soviet Union (Level I: 5) a writer who is critical is sent to a lunatic asylum. In *the* United States (Level I: 5) he is taken to a talk show.

D. Make your choice.

1. b. *Clarity* is the ability to give directions without taking your hands out of your pockets. (Level I:1)
2. b. *The exploration* of space is expected to cost us billions of dollars. (Level I: 1)
3. b. A famous footballer once said that *most of* the people on unemployment are lazy. (Level II: Sprachfallen)

E. Right or wrong?

1. *The specialists* that I work with are people who know everything about nothing and nothing about everything else. (Level I: 1)
2. Bob: I never interfere *with nature*. (Level I :1)
3. The chairman of the Board of Directors once visited one of his directors *in hospital*. (Level II: 7)

F. Translate the German in the brackets.

1. "What did you do *at school* today?" (Level II: 7)
   "Oh," he answers, "in chemistry we made explosives." "And what are you doing at school tomorrow?" Thereupon *little Joe* asks: "At which school?" (Level II: Sprachfallen)
2. When I was young I thought money was *the most important thing* (Level II: Sprachfallen) *in life* (Level I: 1).
3. *Little Billy* (Level I: 4, Level II: Sprachfallen) brought a note home *from school* (Level II: 7).

19

20. Der unbestimmte Artikel – The Indefinite Article

Spot the mistake

a. A filing cabinet is ~~an~~ *a useful* container where things can be lost alphabetically.

b. Ronny was trying to explain to Annette all about nuclear plants. After ~~an half hour~~ *half an hour* she said, "Yes, but what colour are the petals?"

c. A diplomat is a man who can tell you to go to hell in ~~a such~~ *such a way* that you actually look forward to the trip.

d. You are *an alcoholic* if you drink more than your doctor.

Tick them off

	Right	Wrong
a. My boss is *a* conservative. He thinks that nothing should be done for the first time.	✗	
b. My father is *a* teacher. He talks in his pupils' sleep.		✗
c. You're not really ~~a such~~ *such a* bad person – until people get to know you better.		✗
d. What ~~a~~ weather! It's raining cats and dogs.		✗
e. He was a great patriot, ~~an~~ *a* humanitarian, a loyal friend – provided of course he really is dead.		✗

A. Spot the mistakes.

1. Motivation is usually the promise of either a bonus, ~~a~~ *an* assigned parking space (Level 1: 2) or ~~a~~ *an* office with a window. (Level I: 1)

2. You seem to know more and more about less and less, Bob: you're becoming *an* expert. (Level I: 4)

3. He hasn't ~~a~~ *an* enemy in this world and his friends don't like him either. (Level I: 1)

B. Is it *a, an, the* or no Article?

1. "I wish you a happy birthday. May you live to be *a* hundred and then decide if you want to go on." (Level I: 1, Sprachfallen)
2. Psychiatrist: How long have you believed in *reincarnation*?
   Patient: Ever since I was *a* frog. (Level I: 1)
3. The upstairs tenant called to the downstairs tenant:
   "Must you play *the* trumpet all day long? (see Definite Article). If you don't stop I'll go crazy!" – "I'm afraid it's too late," was the reply.
   "I stopped *an* hour ago." (Level I: 3)

C. Which is correct.

1. Ron: I'd like to know how long ~~the~~ *a* human being is able to live without a brain. (Level I: 7)
2. Bob: If only I knew whether to be *a* painter or *a* poet. (Level I: 4)
   Ron: I think you should be *a* poet.
3. Ron: How do you like the change from being a salesman to *a* teacher? (Level I: 4)
4. A manager is *an* ~~a~~ ulcer with authority. (Level I: 1)

D. Complete the exclamations with *an* or *a* where necessary.

1. What *a* day!
2. What *a* fool you are!
3. What weather!
4. What sad news!
4. What *an* awful experience!
5. What interesting information!
6. What *an* intelligent manager!
7. What nonsense!

(Level II: Sprachfallen)

E. Spot the mistakes again.

1. Amy Fernandez works as *a* receptionist at Low Valley Copiers. (Level I: 4)
2. She is a happy girl. What ~~a~~ fun her life could be if she didn't have to work. (Level II: Sprachfallen)
3. After work she goes to the Irish pub where she drinks ~~a half~~ *half a* bottle of wine. (Level II: 9)
4. Anyway, she has enough money. She earns fifty thousand euros ~~the~~ *a* year. (Level II: 8)

F. Now we mix it a bit. Fill in the correct Articles (*a, an, the*), but only if necessary.

David Jones is (1) *an* (Level I: 5) Englishman and (2) *an* (Level I: 4) engineer by profession. I met him during our last term (3) *at* (see Definite Article) university and we soon became close friends. (4) *Life* (Level I: 4) with him was not easy in those days. He had to work as (5) *a* (Level I: 4) waiter at the restaurant opposite (6) *the* (see Definite Article) university during his holidays.

David was very interested in topics like (7) *technical progress* (see Definite Article) and its effects (8) *on* (see Definite Article) *society*. His motto was (9)" *Times* (see Definite Article) have changed and man must change with them. In (10) a (Level II: Sprachfallen) word we must be flexible."

G. Fit in the words in brackets.

1. In Glasgow, Scotland: A wife arrives home from shopping and puts six bottles of whiskey and *half a loaf of bread* (Level II: 9) on the table.
2. Excuse for not coming to the office on a Friday: My aunt hid *quite a large sum* (Level II: 9) of money before she died.

20

21. Adjektiv and Adverb – Adjective and Adverb

Spot the mistake.

a. Peter can run ~~more fast~~ *faster* than me.
b. It was a bad accident and some people were ~~bad~~ *badly* injured.
c. This is a dangerous road, you should drive more ~~careful~~ *carefully*.
d. Tom plays tennis well, but he doesn't always play ~~fairly~~ *fair*.
e. Where is the ~~next~~ *nearest* taxi stand, please?

21

Tick them off.

	Right	Wrong
a. A man who looks you *straight* in the eye and adds a *firm* handshake is hiding something.	✗	
b. It's *hard* to feel fit as a fiddle when you're shaped like a cello.	✗	
c. Comics are fast reading for the ~~slowly~~ *slow* thinking.		✗
d. The thief ran ~~always faster~~ *faster and faster*.		✗

A. Is it *late* or *lately, quick* or *quickly*?

1. Angry boss: Why are you *late* again this morning? (Level I: 1)
2. "Yes," said McGregor, "I've been telephoning Australia *lately*." (Level I: 3, 4)
3. Nothing worth learning is learned *quickly*, except parachuting. (Level I: 3, 4)

B. Spot the mistake.

1. Okay, I'm very angry. I'll come ~~straightly~~ *straight* to the point. (Level I: 1b; von straight gibt es keine Form auf -ly)
2. Advertising may be described as the science of arresting the human intelligence ~~longly~~ *long* enough to get money from it. (Level I: 1)
3. Shoemaker drove much too ~~rapid~~ *rapidly* and was almost killed in a crash. (Level I: 4)

C. It's your choice.

1. When I take a long time – I'm *slow* ~~slowly~~. (Level I: 1)
    When my boss takes a long time – he's *thorough* ~~thoroughly~~. (Level I: 1)
2. Second secretary: "He dresses ~~smart~~ *smartly*." (Level I: 3a, 4)
    First secretary: "And ~~quick~~ *quickly* too!" (Level I: 3a, 4)
3. People who cough *loudly* ~~loud~~ never go to the doctor – they go to the theatre or a concert. (Level I: 3a, 4)

D. Put the word in the brackets into the correct form.

1. Ron: my God, that's the *farthest* you've ever run. (Level I: 7)
2. John: That's the *easiest* exam I've ever done. *(*Level I: 8)
3. Since he has been eating animal fat his arteries have become *narrower* and *narrower*. (Level I: 8)

E. Make your choice.

1. a. An intellectual is a man who has found something *more interesting* than women. (Level I: 5)
2. b. Drive *more slowly* or we'll be killed. (Level I: 6)
3. b. He must be a *highly*-educated person or he wouldn't know all the answers. (Level I: 3 b)

F. Translate the German.

1. A watch is something a woman looks at to see how *late* she is. (Level I: 1b)
2. It must have been *easier* to pass your motor-bike test than it was in my day. I failed it three times. (Level I: 8)
3. School children have a *more interesting* life than we had. They can travel everywhere they want. (Level I: 5)

G. Make your choice.

1. An elderly businessman had problems with his sex life. "You've been working too *hard* ~~hardly~~. Get some exercise," his doctor advised.
    "Try riding a bike a few miles every day." (Level II: 18)
    Two days later the doctor received a phone-call from the man.
    "How are you this morning? Has your sex life improved?" he asked.

"How would I know? I *hardly* ~~hard~~ know where home is. I'm at least fifty miles away," was the angry reply. (Level II: 18)

2. "I was extremely *embarrassed* ~~embarrassing~~ yesterday. I called my wife Sue." (Level II: 17)
   "What's *embarrassing* ~~embarrassed~~ about that?" (Level II: 17)
   "Her name's Anne."
3. My ~~newest~~ *latest* invention is an automatic pancake. You put popcorn in the dough so that it will turn over by itself. (Level II: 17)
4. Lizzie couldn't get a man however ~~hardly~~ *hard* she tried. But one day a gypsy sold her a special Chinese love potion for fifty cents – and it worked. A week later she married the Chinese Ambassador. (Level II: 18)
5. Bob did well in his English test. He came *near* ~~nearly~~ to the top. (Level II: 18)

21

H. Spot the mistake.

1. Anne: Nonsense! I can't really believe that you'll kill yourself if I refuse to go to bed with you. That's ~~ridiculously~~ *ridiculous.* (Level I: 1b)
2. Her hat is a creation that will never go out of style, it will look *ridiculous* year after year. (Level II: 15)
3. The small company got into more *and more* debts. (Level II: 11)

22. Probleme mit Nomen - Problems with Nouns

Spot the mistake

a. A man was found lying in a field with a knife sticking out of his back. The police ~~suspects~~ *suspect* foul play.
b. The Red Indians are worried. The United States ~~want~~ *wants* to give the country back to them.
c. Journalists often have to take risks to get the ~~informations~~ *information* they require.
d. Your presentation has been most entertaining. But are there ~~some~~ *any* hard facts to follow?
e. Our President is a man of ~~little~~ *few* words. Unfortunately he keeps repeating them.

Tick them off

Right   Wrong

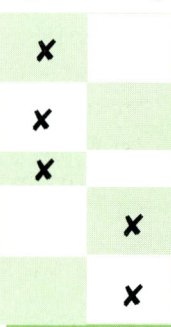

a. In Marseille the government is trying to stop gambling. Many officers are bankrupt.
b. Australia – a country where men are men, and sheep are nervous.
c. The news is never very good nowadays.
d. The room was so full of ~~furnitures~~ *furniture* it was difficult to move.
e. Lots of ~~persons~~ *people* confuse bad management with destiny.

A. Make your choice.

1. a   Ron: Doctor, doctor, *lots of* my hair fell out while I was brushing it this morning. (Level I: 4c)
2. b   Bob: Now that you are married, may I give you *some* (Level I: 4c) advice? Take out *some* insurance. (Level I: 4c)
3. b   We all know that a cat has nine *lives*. (Level I: 2b)

B. Translate the German in the brackets.

1. "There are no *fish* under the ice!" the voice boomed. (Level I: 2a)
2. He ought to go to a dentist and have some *wisdom teeth* put in. (Level I: 2b)
3. A man's credit card was stolen, but he decided not to tell the police because the thief was spending *less* money than his wife did. (Level I: 4b)

C. Which is correct?

1. Call a meeting at 4:30 p.m. on Friday and you'll get ~~few~~ *little* opposition. (Level I: 4b)
2. ~~Thiefs~~ *Thieves* escaped with over 600,000 pounds in a robbery in Glasgow. (Level I: 2b)
3. There's ~~many~~ *a lot of* (Level I: 4c) ~~pigs~~ *pork* (Level I: 3) on that plate.

D. Spot the mistakes.

1. The best ~~advices~~ *advice* (Level II: 5b) I was ever given was on my twenty-first birthday when my father said, "son, here's a million dollars. Don't lose it."
2. Annette arrived in Hong Kong and she hated it. There were far too many ~~peoples~~ *people* (Level II: Sprachfallen) on the streets.
3. You have two cows; the government ~~take~~ *takes* (Level II: 6b) both and ~~sell~~ *sells* (Level II: 6b) you the milk.

E. Translate the German in the brackets.

1. Definition of a lecture: a means of transferring *information* (Level II: 5b) from the notes of the lecturer to the notes of the student without passing through the minds of either.
2. "Can you give me *a pair of scissors*? (Level II: 5a) I need to cut this bankcard up."
3. *The police are* (Level II: 6a) all under-equipped. Moreover, *they don't carry any* (Level II: 6a) weapons in the U.K.

F. Make your choice.

At Frank's flat. Silvia and Frank:

F: Hi, Silvia. I haven't seen you for ages.

S: So this is your new place. I must say it's in ~~a very nice surrounding~~ *very nice surroundings.* (Level II: 5c)

22

F: Yes, but it's very expensive here in Heidelberg. Two thousand Euros *is* ~~are~~ too much to pay. (Level II: Sprachfallen)

S: I'm afraid that's the same for all of us. The local government *is* ~~are~~ only interested in robbing the population to pay for stupid things that we all don't need. (Level II: 6b)

F: You're right and my *wages are* ~~wage is~~ simply too small to cover this rent and all the extra costs. (Level II: 5c)

The A, B, C of Grammar

Adjective

in front of nouns	a *bad* choice, a *clever* girl, the *red* car
after be	she's *crazy*, he's *rich*, they were *late*
as nouns	the *unemployed*, the *rich*
comparative	he's *taller than* me, she's *more intelligent than* you. we're *better* runners, the *worse* alternative
irregulars	we're *the tallest*, he's *the friendliest* person
superlative	she's *the best*, he's *the worst*, it's *the farthest* away, that costs the most
irregulars	

Adverbs

of time	today, yesterday, tomorrow, last week etc.
of place	backwards, close, far, everywhere, over there
of manner	stupidly, badly, easily, happily
irregulars	good → well, fast → fast, hard → hard
restriction adverbs	hardly, scarcely, never, only, rarely, seldom
comparative	harder, deeper, faster, more often, more
irregulars	he did it *well / worse*, I have *more* wine, give me *further* information
superlative	it was *the hardest / slowest / earliest*, she shouted *the most happily*
irregulars	he works *best / worst*, she writes *most carefully*

Articles

Definite Article

to specify	You know *the* person I'm talking about.
the & adjective	*the* sick, *the* unemployed
no definite article	See you at *Christmas*. We'll meet in *spring*.

Indefinite Article

job, religion nationality	He's *a* Catholic. She's *a* Norwegian.
exclamations	What *a* beautiful girl!

The A, B, C of Grammar

Conditionals

Type I	*If* you *give* me the money, I'*ll buy* it.
Type II	*If* you *gave* me the money, I'*d buy* it.
	(If you *were to give* me the money, I'd *buy* it.)
Type III	*If* you *had given* me the money, I *would have bought* it. (*Had* you *given* me the money, I *would have bought* it).

Gerund

as subject	*Swimming* keeps your bones and joints loose.
as object and after certain verbs	I avoid *seeing* her nowadays / he *enjoys drinking* wine.
after prepositions	We're thinking *of finding* a new apartment.
Gerund or to (same meaning)	It continued *to rain* / it continued *raining*.
Gerund or to (different meaning)	He *went on talking* / he *went on to talk* about. She *stopped shouting* / she *stopped to open* her briefcase.
verbs followed by Gerunds	avoid, consider deny, enjoy, excuse, finish, imagine, mind, miss, postpone, practise, risk, suggest

Imperative

with "do"	*Do sit* down. *Do join* us this evening.
with "let's"	*Let's* go to the party. *Let's* not argue about Bob.

Infinitive with "to"

purpose	I've come *to tell* you what I think.
verbs plus Infinitive with "to"	agree to come, intend to meet, begin to laugh, learn to read, decide to leave, love to travel, forget to do, need to speak, help to survive, promise to wait, hope to see, refuse to go, want to visit, seem to understand, wish to stay, try to help

Infinitive without "to"

make, let	He *made* him *wash* the car. He *let* him *have* the car.
verbs plus Infinitive without "to"	see, hear, watch, notice, feel
verbs of perception	I *saw* him come. We *heard* him cry.

Indirect Speech

introduced by Present	Bob *says he wants* to leave the country.
introduced by Past	Ron *noticed that* he had forgotten his money.
converting direct into indirect Modals	"I'm eating" → He *said he was eating.*
	"We will do it" → They *said (that) they would do* it.
Imperatives	"Close your book!" → He *told me to close* my book.
	→ He *said I should close* my book.

Linking Words

time	now that, before, when, as soon as, once, whenever, while, after
future time	after, as, as soon as, before, until (till), when, while
reason	that's why, as, because, since
result	as a result, consequently, such that, therefore, so that
contrast	but, on the other hand, even though, although however, whereas, while, though
purpose	so as to, so that, in order that, in order to
comparison	as ... as, not as ... as, not so ... as, ... than

The A, B, C of Grammar

Nouns

regular plural	two boys, three Euros, a lot of cars
irregulars	children, mice, woman, geese, surroundings
mostly plural	earnings, scales, scissors
mostly singular	advice, business, furniture, information, knowledge
singular = plural	sheep, fish, salmon, deer, police, government
Nouns and possessive	John's place, my parent's house
(genitive)	half a bottle, glass of lemonade
compound Nouns	boy-friend, mother-in-law, spoonful

Numerals

cardinals	1st, 2nd, 3rd – first, second, third
ordinals	once, twice, three times
fractions	1/2, 1/3, 1/4, – a half, a third, a quarter
decimals	2.6, 3.7 – two point six, three point seven

Phrasal Verbs

general	I was *turned down* after my interview.
two particles	She's on holiday. You'll have to *stand in for* her.

Pronouns

personal	*I* think, we know, *he / she / it* has, *they* want
general	*one, you* → one could print it, you could say that
possessive pronoun	That book is *mine, yours, hers, his, ours, theirs.*
possessive adjective	*your* cat, *her* dog, *his* joke, *our* loss, *their* stupidity
double possessive	He's a friend *of mine / yours / hers / his / ours / theirs.*
reciprocal	We haven't seen *each other* for years.
demonstrative	*These* are my books, *those* are your books, *that* is my car.
demonstrative adjective	*that* book, *this* money, *those* boys, *these* idiots
relative	the job *that* you got, the man *whose* car was stolen, the suit *which* I bought last week

emphatic	We can build it *ourselves*, you *yourself* should do it – myself, yourself, himself, herself, itself, ourselves, yourselves, themselves
verb & reflexive	You didn't *behave yourself*. We *worked ourselves* to death.
indefinite	somebody, someone, something anybody, anyone, anything nobody, noone, nothing everybody, everyone, everything

Prepositions

place	I live *near* a very nice hotel.
time	Jenny intends to stay *until* December next year.
others	*Despite* the weather we'll play football.
verbs & preps	We can't *agree on* a colour scheme for he room.

Question Tags

general	I met you there, *didn't I?* We didn't argue then, *did we?*
ironic / aggressive tags	Oh, *you won't, won't you?* Oh, *you will, will you?*

Tenses

Present Progressive	Ann *is sleeping*, Tom *is lying*, we *are worrying*
Present Progressive with always	he's *always complaining*, she's *forever forgetting*
Present Simple	I *do* it often, we rarely *speak*, they never *play*
stative verbs	I *know / like / hear / understand* you
Past Simple	yesterday we *had* money, two days ago she *left* him
Past Progressive	he *was waiting* by the phone, they *were thinking* about it all day
Present Perfect (complete)	I *have visited* Afghanistan, she *has worked* very hard
Present Perfect (incomplete)	I *have lived* here *for* ten years, she *has known* that *since* yesterday

The A, B, C of Grammar

for / since **Present Perfect Progressive**	They*'ve been playing* football for two hours / since 1999. What on earth *have* you *been doing*, your clothes are torn.
Past Perfect	I *had left* the company before she arrived.
Past Perfect Progressive	We *had been waiting* for an hour before she arrived.
Will-Future	I*'ll give* you the answer tomorrow. He*'ll take* his holiday in India.
Going to-Future	I*'m going to* pass the exam if I can.
Present Progressive for Future	Yes, we*'re leaving* early *tomorrow* morning.
Future Progressive	They*'ll be lying* on the beach by now.
Future Perfect	She *will have left* the country before they find the body.
Present Simple for Future (timetable)	The plane *leaves* at ten o'clock every day.

Irregular Verbs

Grundform Infinitive	1. Vergangenheit (Imperfekt / Past Simple)	2. Vergangenheit (Partizip Perfekt / have-form)	German
arise	arose	arisen	*entstehen*
awake	awoke	awoken	*aufwachen*
be	was, were	been	*sein*
beat	beat	beat	*schlagen*
become	became	become	*werden*
begin	began	begun	*beginnen*
bend	bent	bent	*biegen*
bet*	bet	bet	*wetten*
bid	bid	bid	*bieten*
bind	bound	bound	*binden*
bite	bit	bitten	*beißen*
bleed	bled	bled	*bluten*
blow	blew	blown	*blasen*
break	broke	broken	*brechen*
breed	bred	bred	*brüten, züchten*
bring	brought	brought	*bringen*
broadcast	broadcast	broadcast	*senden, übertragen (Radio, Fernsehen)*
build	built	built	*bauen*
burn*	burnt	burnt	*brennen*
burst	burst	burst	*bersten*
buy	bought	bought	*kaufen*
cast	cast	cast	*gießen*
catch	caught	caught	*fangen*
choose	chose	chosen	*wählen*
cling	clung	clung	*sich klammen an*
come	came	come	*kommen*
cost	cost	cost	*kosten*

creep	crept	crept	*kriechen*
cut	cut	cut	*schneiden*
deal	dealt	dealt	*handeln*
dig	dug	dug	*graben*
do	did	done	*tun*
draw	drew	drawn	*ziehen, zeichnen*
dream*	dreamt	dreamt	*träumen*
drink	drank	drunk	*trinken*
drive	drove	driven	*fahren*
eat	ate	eaten	*essen*
fall	fell	fallen	*fallen*
feed	fed	fed	*füttern*
feel	felt	felt	*fühlen*
fight	fought	fought	*kämpfen*
find	found	found	*finden*
fling	flung	flung	*schleudern*
fly	flew	flown	*fliegen*
forbid	forbade, forbad	forbidden	*verbieten*
forecast	forecast	forecast	*vorhersagen*
forget	forgot	forgotten	*vergessen*
forgive	forgave	forgiven	*vergeben*
freeze	froze	frozen	*frieren*
get	got	got	*bekommen*
give	gave	given	*geben*
go	went	gone (been)	*gehen*
grind	ground	ground	*schleifen*
grow	grew	grown	*wachsen*
hang*	hung	hung	*aufhängen*
have	had	had	*haben*
hear	heard	heard	*hören*
hide	hid	hidden	*verstecken*
hit	hit	hit	*treffen*
hold	held	held	*halten*
hurt	hurt	hurt	*verletzen*
keep	kept	kept	*behalten*
kneel*	knelt	knelt	*knien*

knit*	knit	knit	*stricken*
know	knew	known	*wissen, kennen*
lay	laid	laid	*legen*
lead	led	led	*führen*
lean*	leant	leant	*lehnen*
leap*	leapt	leapt	*springen*
learn*	learnt	learnt	*lernen*
leave	left	left	*verlassen*
lend	lent	lent	*leihen*
let	let	let	*lassen*
lie	lay	lain	*lügen*
light*	lit	lit	*anzünden*
lose	lost	lost	*verlieren*
make	made	made	*machen*
mean	meant	meant	*meinen*
meet	met	met	*treffen*
mistake	mistook	mistaken	*verwechseln*
misunderstand	misunderstood	misunderstood	*missverstehen*
mow	mowed	mown	*mähen*
overcome	overcame	overcome	*überwinden*
pay	paid	paid	*(be-)zahlen*
put	put	put	*legen*
quit*	quit	quit	*aufgeben, kündigen*
read	read	read	*lesen*
rid	rid	rid	*befreien, loswerden*
ride	rode	ridden	*reiten*
ring	rang	rung	*läuten*
rise	rose	risen	*sich erheben, aufstehen*
run	ran	run	*rennen*
saw	sawed	sawn	*sägen*
say	said	said	*sagen*
see	saw	seen	*sehen*
seek	sought	sought	*suchen*
sell	sold	sold	*verkaufen*
send	sent	sent	*(ver-)senden*
set	set	set	*setzen, stellen, legen*

Unregelmäßige Verben

sew	sewed	sewn	*nähen*
shake	shook	shaken	*zittern*
shed	shed	shed	*verschütten*
shine	shone	shone	*scheinen*
shoot	shot	shot	*schießen*
show	shown	showed	*zeigen*
shrink	shrank	shrunk	*schrumpfen*
shut	shut	shut	*schließen*
sing	sang	sung	*singen*
sink	sank	sunk	*sinken*
sit	sat	sat	*sitzen*
sleep	slept	slept	*schlafen*
slide	slid	slid	*gleiten*
sling	slung	slung	*schleudern*
slink	slunk	slunk	*schleichen*
slit	slit	slit	*aufschlitzen*
smell*	smelt	smelt	*riechen*
sow	sowed	sown	*säen*
speak	spoke	spoken	*sprechen*
speed*	sped	sped	*beschleunigen*
spell*	spelt	spelt	*buchstabieren*
spend	spent	spent	*ausgeben*
spill*	spilt	spilt	*verschütten*
spin	spun, span	spun	*spinnen*
spit	spat	spat	*spucken*
split	split	split	*spalten*
spoil*	spoilt	spoilt	*verderben*
spread	spread	spread	*verbreiten*
spring	sprang	sprung	*springen*
stand	stood	stood	*stehen*
steal	stole	stolen	*stehlen*
stick	stuck	stuck	*stecken*
sting	stung	stung	*stechen*
sink	stank	stunk	*sinken*
stride	strode	stridden	*schreiten*
strike	struck	struck	*schlagen*
string	strung	strung	*spannen, zubinden*

strive	strove	striven	*streben*
swear	swore	sworn	*schwören*
sweat*	sweat	sweat	*schwitzen*
sweep	swept	swept	*kehren*
swell	swelled	swollen	*anschwellen*
swim	swam	swum	*schwimmen*
swing	swung	swung	*schwingen*
take	took	taken	*nehmen*
teach	taught	taught	*lehren*
tear	tore	torn	*reißen*
tell	told	told	*sagen, erzählen*
think	thought	thought	*denken*
throw	threw	thrown	*werfen*
thrust	thrust	thrust	*stoßen*
tread	trod	trodden	*treten*
understand	understood	understood	*verstehen*
undertake	undertook	undertaken	*übernehmen*
upset	upset	upset	*umwerfen*
wake	woke	woken	*wachen*
wear	wore	worn	*tragen, anhaben*
weave	wove	woven	*weben*
weep	wept	wept	*weinen*
wet	wet	wet	*anfeuchten*
win	won	won	*gewinnen*
wind	wound	wound	*winden, wickeln*
withdraw	withdrew	withdrawn	*zurückziehen*
withhold	withheld	withheld	*zurückhalten*
withstand	withstood	withstood	*widerstehen*
wring	wrung	wrung	*wringen*
write	wrote	written	*schreiben*

Die mit * markierten Verben haben auch eine regelmäßige Form, die mit -ed endet. Im Falle von *hang* ändert sich zugleich die Bedeutung:

He hung the picture on the wall → ein Bild aufhängen (für Objekte)
They hanged him from a tree → an einem Baum aufhängen (zum Töten)

Unregelmäßige Verben

Infinitive	Past Simple	Past Participle (für Present Perfect, Past Perfect, Future Perfect und Passive)	German
bet	betted	betted	*wetten*
burn	burned	burned	*brennen*
dream	dreamed	dreamed	*träumen*
hang	hanged	hanged	*hängen*
kneel	kneeled	kneeled	*knien*
knit	knitted	knitted	*stricken*
lean	leaned	leaned	*lehnen*
leap	leaped	leaped	*springen*
learn	learned	learned	*lernen*
light	lighted	lighted	*anzünden*
quit	quitted	quitted	*aufgeben, kündigen*
smell	smelled	smelled	*riechen*
speed	speeded	speeded	*beschleunigen*
spell	spelled	spelled	*buchstabieren*
spill	spilled	spilled	*verschütten*
spoil	spoiled	spoiled	*verderben*
sweat	sweated	sweated	*schwitzen*

ability	*Fähigkeit*
absent-minded	*zerstreut, geistesabwesend*
accelerator	*Gaspedal*
accident	*Unfall*
accountant	*Buchhalter*
acquaintance	*Bekannte(r)*
act	*schauspielern, handeln*
acute	*akut*
adultery	*Ehebruch*
advance; in ~	*im Voraus*
advertising space	*Werbefläche*
advice	*Rat*
advise	*raten*
afford something	*sich etwas leisten*
algebra	*Algebra*
annual costs	*jährliche Kosten*
apart	*getrennt*
appendix	*Blinddarm*
appointment	*Termin, Verabredung*
appropriate	*angemessen*
argue	*streiten*
art critic	*Kunstkritiker*
artificial	*künstlich*
artificial respiration	*künstliche Beatmung*
assigned parking space	*zugewiesener Parkplatz*
attendance	*Anwesenheit*
attention	*Aufmerksamkeit*
autumn	*Herbst*
awake	*wach*
bark	*bellen*
battle	*Schlacht*
beat eggs	*Eier schlagen*

Word Aid

beautician	*Kosmetiker*
bee	*Biene*
beer	*Bier*
behaviour	*Verhalten, Benehmen*
behind	*hier: der Hintern*
belch	*rülpsen*
bell	*Glocke*
big-game	*Großwild*
black eye	*blaues Auge*
blame someone	*jemandem die Schuld geben*
bloke	*Kerl, Bursche*
blurred	*verschwommen*
board game	*Brettspiel*
boot	*Stiefel*
bore	*Langweiler*
borrow something	*sich etwas leihen*
bow	*sich verbeugen*
bracket	*Klammer*
brain	*Gehirn*
breast-stroke	*Brustschwimmen*
bridegroom	*Bräutigam*
bright	*schlau, intelligent*
browse	*stöbern*
bulb	*Glühbirne*
bury	*begraben*
button	*Knopf*
calculator	*Taschenrechner*
call it a day	*Schluss / Feierabend machen*
canary	*Kanarienvogel*
cancel	*stornieren, löschen*
capital	*Hauptstadt*
catch a train	*einen Zug erreichen*
ceiling	*Decke*
chance	*Glück, Zufall*
chancellor	*Kanzler*
chase	*jagen*

cheek	*Backe*
chess	*Schach*
choice	*Wahl*
civil servant	*Beamte(r)*
cleaning lady	*Putzfrau*
coffin	*Sarg*
coincidence	*Zufall*
collapse	*einstürzen*
collection plate	*Klingelbeutel*
commandment	*Gebot*
commit adultery	*Ehebruch begehen*
compartment	*Abteil*
competition	*Wettbewerb*
complain	*sich beschweren*
confuse	*verwechseln*
connection	*Verbindung*
conscience	*Gewissen*
consider	*betrachten, erwägen*
consist of	*bestehen aus*
contain	*enthalten*
continually	*ständig*
continuation of the species	*Fortbestand der Arten*
convince	*überzeugen*
cough	*husten; Husten*
count	*zählen*
coward	*Feigling*
crawl	*kriechen*
cremate	*einäschern*
Crete	*Kreta*
cross	*Kreuzung*
cure	*heilen, Heilung*
customer	*Kunde*
deaf	*taub*
debts	*Schulden*
decide	*entscheiden, beschließen*
decrease	*abnehmen, geringer werden*

depend on	*abhängen von*
deposit	*Einlage, Einzahlung*
deposit in an account	*in ein Konto einzahlen*
deserve	*verdienen*
destiny	*Schicksal*
destroy	*zerstören*
dignity	*Würde*
directions	*Anweisungen*
disappear	*verschwinden*
disappoint	*enttäuschen*
disconcerting	*peinlich, beunruhigend*
disease	*Krankheit*
disgust somebody	*jemanden anekeln*
distant relative	*entfernte(r) Verwandte(r)*
disturb	*stören*
divorce	*Scheidung, sich scheiden lassen*
dodgy	*zweifelhaft, nicht einwandfrei, vertrackt*
dough	*Teig*
dream	*träumen*
driving licence	*Führerschein*
drown	*ertrinken*
eagle	*Adler*
Easter	*Ostern*
economics	*Wirtschaftswissenschaften*
edge	*Rand*
Egypt	*Ägypten*
electricity supply	*Stromzufuhr, -versorgung*
embarrassing	*peinlich*
enduring	*dauerhaft*
enemy	*Feind*
enjoy	*sich amüsieren, genießen*
enlarge	*vergrößern*
enquire	*fragen, sich erkundigen*
equip	*ausrüsten*
ensure	*gewährleisten*
erase	*löschen, ausradieren*

error	*Irrtum*
escalator	*Rolltreppe*
escape	*fliehen, entgehen*
evidence	*Beweis(e)*
except	*außer*
excuse	*entschuldigen*
executive	*leitender Angestellter*
exercise	*Übung; Bewegung*
experience	*Erfahrung*
face someone	*entgegentreten*
failure	*Misserfolg*
faint	*ohnmächtig werden*
fake	*vortäuschen, fälschen*
father-in-law	*Schwiegervater*
fault	*Fehler*
feather	*Feder*
fed up, be ~~ with	*die Nase voll haben von*
filing cabinet	*Aktenschrank*
firearm	*Schusswaffe*
fireplace	*Kamin*
firing squad	*Erschießungskommando*
firm	*fest; Firma*
flour	*Mehl*
fly	*Fliege*
fly, flew, flown	*fliegen*
forehead	*Stirn*
formerly	*früher*
fur coat	*Pelzmantel*
gain	*gewinnen*
garbage	*Abfall*
gate	*Tor*
genius	*Genie*
get something straight	*etwas klarstellen*
ghost	*Gespenst*
glove	*Handschuh*
go to court	*vor Gericht klagen*

Word Aid

golf club	*Golfschläger, Golfklub*
goose, geese	*Gans, Gänse*
gossip	*Klatsch*
grow	*wachsen*
guilty	*schuldig*
guy	*Bursche*
gypsy	*Zigeuner*
hall	*Flur*
handrail	*Geländer, Handlauf*
handshake	*Händedruck*
handsome	*stattlich, ansehnlich*
harbour	*Hafen*
hate	*hassen*
headmaster	*Schulleiter*
healer	*Heiler*
hedgehog	*Igel*
hesitate	*zögern*
hole	*Loch*
honest	*ehrlich*
honeymoon	*Flitterwochen*
horseradish	*Meerrettich*
hug	*umarmen, an sich drücken*
hurt	*wehtun*
hush up	*vertuschen*
ice cube	*Eiswürfel*
ice rink	*Eislaufhalle*
ill	*Leiden, Krankheit; krank*
illiterate person	*Analphabet*
imagination	*Phantasie*
imagine	*sich vorstellen*
income tax	*Einkommensteuer*
increase	*zunehmen, größer werden*
incredible	*unglaublich*
injure	*verletzen*
injured	*verletzt*
innocent	*unschuldig*

insist on	*bestehen auf*
insurance agent / salesman	*Versicherungsvertreter*
interfere with	*sich einmischen in*
interrupt	*unterbrechen*
introduce	*vorstellen, einführen*
jealous	*eifersüchtig*
kiss of life	*Mund-zu-Mund-Beatmung*
last a lifetime	*ein ganzes Leben anhalten*
laundry	*Wäscherei*
law	*Gesetz*
lawyer	*Rechtsanwalt*
lecture	*Vorlesung*
lemon	*Zitrone*
lend	*(ver-) leihen*
less	*weniger*
letter	*Buchstabe; Brief*
licence	*Führerschein*
light bulb	*Glühbirne*
limitation	*Einschränkung*
lively	*lebhaft*
liver	*Leber*
local	*Einheimischer*
long-term	*langfristig*
lose	*verlieren*
lose weight	*abnehmen*
lousy	*lausig, erbärmlich*
lunatic asylum	*Irrenanstalt*
mad	*verrückt, tollwütig*
mailing list	*Postverteiler*
make fun of	*sich lustig machen über*
make one's mind up	*sich entscheiden*
map	*Atlas, Karte*
marriage	*Ehe*
marriage counselling	*Eheberatung*
marry	*heiraten*
medical check-up	*ärztliche Untersuchung*

Word Aid

mental hospital	*psychiatrisches Krankenhaus*
message	*Botschaft, Nachricht*
mind	*etwas dagegen haben; Geist*
Minister of Defence	*Verteidigungsminister*
mistress	*Geliebte*
moan	*jammern*
moderation	*Mäßigung, Maß*
monkey	*Affe*
mutton	*Hammelfleisch*
nag	*kritisieren, nörgeln*
narrow	*eng*
national debt	*Staatsschulden*
native	*Eingeborene(r)*
next door	*nebenan*
nibble	*Biss (beim Fischen)*
noise	*Geräusch, Lärm*
note	*Mitteilung*
notorious	*bekannt, berüchtigt*
novelist	*Romanschriftsteller*
nuclear plant	*Atomkraftwerk*
nut	*Nuss*
omnipotence	*Allmacht*
operator	*Telefondame*
opinion	*Meinung*
order	*Auftrag; Befehl*
other; the other day	*neulich*
overestimate	*überschätzen*
own	*besitzen*
oyster	*Auster*
pancake	*Pfannkuchen*
paper	*Test, Klassenarbeit*
parachute	*Fallschirm*
parachuting	*Fallschirmspringen*
parrot	*Papagei*
pavement	*Gehsteig*
pay attention	*aufmerken, aufpassen*

pedestrian	*Fußgänger*
permission	*Erlaubnis*
petrol tank	*Benzintank*
plane	*Flugzeug*
plant	*Pflanze*
plumber	*Klempner*
poisonous	*giftig*
Pole	*Pole, (Nord-)Pol*
policy	*Strategie, Politik*
population	*Bevölkerung*
possess	*besitzen*
postponement	*Aufschub, Verschiebung*
potion	*Trank*
pour	*gießen*
practice jump	*Übungssprung*
praise	*loben; Lob*
pram	*Kinderwagen*
pray	*beten*
precipice	*Abgrund*
pregnant	*schwanger*
price	*Preis (den man bezahlt)*
prize	*Preis (den man gewinnt)*
procedure	*Verfahren; Vorgehensweise*
promise	*versprechen*
proof	*Beweis*
properly	*richtig, passend, wie es sich gehört*
provided	*vorausgesetzt, dass ...*
provoke	*provozieren, reizen*
publisher	*Verleger*
pull faces	*Gesichter schneiden*
pull oneself together	*sich zusammenreißen*
put off	*aufschieben*
put to sleep	*einschläfern*
put up with	*sich begnügen mit*
rabies	*Tollwut*
raise	*Gehaltserhöhung*

Word Aid

reception desk	*Empfang*
rectangular	*rechteckig*
referee	*Schiedsrichter*
refrigerator	*Kühlschrank*
refuse	*sich weigern, ablehnen*
reincarnation	*Wiedergeburt*
related	*verwandt*
relative	*Verwandte(r)*
reliability	*Zuverlässigkeit*
remain	*bleiben*
remark	*Bemerkung*
replace	*ersetzen*
reply	*Antwort*
request	*Bitte, Verlangen, Forderung*
require	*erfordern, erbitten, benötigen*
rib	*Rippe*
ridiculous	*lächerlich*
road safety notice	*Verkehrswarnschild*
rock	*Stein, Felsen*
rod	*(Angel-) Rute*
rule	*Regel*
rumour	*Gerücht*
run	*leiten*
sample	*Muster*
sausage	*Wurst*
scarf, scarves	*Halstuch, Halstücher*
scream	*schreien, kreischen*
screen	*Bildschirm*
secret	*geheim; Geheimnis*
self-preservation	*Selbsterhaltung*
sensitive	*empfindlich*
share	*Anteil*
share the blame	*die Schuld teilen*
shelf	*Regal*
short cut	*Abkürzung*
short hand	*Steno*

shower	*Dusche*
sigh	*seufzen*
silk	*Seide*
size	*Größe*
slap someone's face	*jemandem eine Ohrfeige geben*
smart	*schlau*
sober	*nüchtern*
speech	*Rede, Sprache*
speeding	*zu schnelles Fahren*
spicy	*gewürzt*
spill	*verschütten*
spit	*spucken*
splinter	*Splitter*
spoon	*Löffel*
sprain one's ankle	*sich den Knöchel verstauchen*
spread gossip	*Gerüchte verbreiten*
spring a leak	*undicht werden*
spy	*Spion; spionieren*
stab	*erstechen*
stand the climate	*das Klima aushalten*
steady; a ~job	*ein sicherer Beruf*
stock	*Aktien*
stock exchange	*(Aktien-)Börse*
straight	*gerade*
stutter	*Stottern*
submarine	*Unterseeboot*
success	*Erfolg*
suffering	*Leiden*
suggest	*vorschlagen, anregen*
suggestion	*Vorschlag*
suitable	*passend*
suitcase	*Koffer*
sunset	*Sonnenuntergang*
swallow	*verschlucken*
swan	*Schwan*
tablet	*Tafel, Tablette*

Word Aid

take notice of	*bemerken, wahrnehmen*
taste	*Geschmack*
tear, tore, torn	*zerreißen*
tenant	*Mieter*
tender	*zart*
tent	*Zelt*
thorough	*gründlich*
throne	*Thron*
ticket inspector	*Kontrolleur*
tight	*eng*
tiring	*ermüdend*
tongue	*Zunge*
trade union	*Gewerkschaft*
truck	*Lastwagen*
trust	*vertrauen*
truth	*Wahrheit*
tune	*stimmen (Klavier)*
twice	*zweimal*
twins	*Zwillinge*
ugly	*hässlich*
ulcer	*Magengeschwür*
umbrella	*Regenschirm*
undertaker	*Leichenbestatter*
unemployment	*Arbeitslosigkeit*
Valentines	*Geschenk zum Valentinstag*
valuable	*wertvoll*
virgin	*Jungfrau*
waitress	*Bedienung*
wake, woke, woken	*wecken*
wallet	*Brieftasche*
warehouse	*Warenlager*
wash the dishes	*abspülen*
waste time	*Zeit verschwenden*
weather forecast	*Wetterbericht*
weight	*Gewicht*
well-behaved	*manierlich*

willpower	*Willenskraft*
wing	*Flügel*
wisdom tooth	*Weisheitszahn*
wonder	*sich fragen, sich wundern*
worry	*sich Sorgen machen*
wriggle	*zappeln*
wrinkled	*faltig, verrunzelt*
xenophobe	*Fremdenhasser*

Geschäftsbesuche, Briefe, Telefonate, Verhandlungen und Meetings verlangen ein klares sprachliches Konzept. Die Serie **Business Englisch** von **René Bosewitz** und **Robert Kleinschroth** hilft praxisnah und übersichtlich in allen Standardsituationen: mit griffigen Dialogen und informativen Texten, mit didaktisch ausgereiften Übungen und nicht zuletzt mit viel Witz.

René Bosewitz/Robert Kleinschroth
Better than the Boss
Business English fürs Büro
3-499-60138-9

René Bosewitz/Robert Kleinschroth
Better Your Business Englisch
*Crashprogramm zum Meistern
typischer Probleme*
3-499-608464-4/61448-0

René Bosewitz/Robert Kleinschroth
Check Your Language Level
Business English auf dem Prüfstand
3-499-60268-7

René Bosewitz/Robert Kleinschroth
Get Through at Meetings
*Business English für Konferenzen
und Präsentationen*
3-499-60262-8

René Bosewitz/Robert Kleinschroth
Get Through at Meetings
*Business English für Konferenzen
und Präsentationen.
Buch mit Audio-CD*
3-499-60265-2

3-499-61448-0

René Bosewitz/Robert Kleinschroth
Get Through at Meetings
*Business English für Konferenzen
und Präsentationen.
Buch mit Tonkassette*
3-499-60266-0

René Bosewitz/Robert Kleinschroth
How to Communicate Effectively
*Verstehen und verstanden werden
im Business*
3-499-61146-5

René Bosewitz/Robert Kleinschroth
How to Phone Effectively
Business English am Telefon.
3-499-60139-7/61449-9
Buch mit Audio-CD
3-499-60146-X/64156-1
Buch mit Tonkassette
3-499-60147-8

René Bosewitz/Robert Kleinschroth
Idioms at Work
*Bessere Geschäfte
mit treffendem Englisch*
3-499-61333-6

René Bosewitz/Robert Kleinschroth
Manage in English
Business rund um die Firma
3-499-60137-0

René Bosewitz/Robert Kleinschroth
Master Your Business Phrases
Sprachmodule für den Geschäftsalltag
3-499-60725-5

3-499-61146-X

Illustration: Cathrin Günther

René Bosewitz/Robert Kleinschroth
Small Talk for Big Business
Business Conversation für
bessere Kontakte
Buch mit Tonkassette
3-499-60578-3
Buch mit Audio-CD
3-499-60577-5/61455-3

René Bosewitz/Robert Kleinschroth
Get to Grips with Company English
Wortschatztraining on the job
3-499-60845-6

René Bosewitz/Robert Kleinschroth
Spice up Your Speeches
Rhetorik für alle Geschäftsanlässe
3-499-60804-9
Buch mit Tonkassette
3-499-60844-8
Buch mit Audio-CD
3-499-60843-X

René Bosewitz/Robert Kleinschroth
The Way Things Work
Technisches English für Business
und Alltag
3-499-60369-1

3-499-60804-9

Illustration: Gerd Huss

Gunther Bischoff
Better Times
Ein leichtes Programm zum richtigen
Gebrauch der englischen Zeiten
3-499-17987-3

Gunther Bischoff
Speak you English
Programmierte Übung zum Verlernen
typisch deutscher Englischfehler
3-499-16857-X

René Bosewitz
Better Your English
Wie man typische deutsche Fehler
verlernt
3-499-60802-2

René Bosewitz
Perfect Your English
Wie man die typischsten Sprachfallen
vermeidet
3-499-61147-3

Hartmut Breitkreuz
False Friends
Stolpersteine des
deutsch-englischen Wortschatzes
3-499-18492-3

Emer O'Sullivan/DietmarRösler
Modern Talking
Englisches Quasselbuch mit Sprüchen
und Widersprüchen
3-499-18427-3

3-499-61147-3

Illustration: Gerd Huss

Iain Gailbraith/Paul Krieger
English in letzter Minute
Sprachkurs für Überflieger
Hg. von Christof Kehr
3-499-60908-8

Iain Gailbraith/Paul Krieger
English in letzter Minute
Sprachkurs für Überflieger
Buch mit Audio-CD
Hg. von Christof Kehr
3-499-60909-6

Iain Gailbraith/Paul Krieger
English in letzter Minute
Sprachkurs für Überflieger
Hg. von Christof Kehr
Buch mit Tonkassette
3-499-60910-X

Hans-Georg Heuber
Talk one's head off.
Ein Loch in den Bauch reden
Englische Redewendungen und ihre
deutschen «opposite numbers»
3-499-17653-X

Ronald Lister/Klemens Veth
Idioms im Griff
Phrasal Verbes, Redewendungen und
Metaphern nach Situationen
3-499-60507-4

Ernest Pasakarnis
Master Your Idioms
Der Schlüssel zu den englischen
Redewendungen
3-499-18491-5

3-499-60909-6